Focus on the Fabulous

FOCUS ON THE

COLORADO
GLBT VOICES

Edited by
Matt Kailey

JOHNSON BOOKS • BOULDER

Published by Johnson Books, a Big Earth Publishing company,
3005 Center Green Drive, Suite 220, Boulder, Colorado 80301.
E-mail: books@bigearthpublishing.com
www.bigearthpublishing.com
1-800-258-5830

Cover and text design by Polly Christensen
Cover photo © Tom Pretto

9   8   7   6   5   4   3   2   1

Library of Congress Cataloging-in-Publication Data

Focus on the fabulous: Colorado GLBT voices / edited by Matt Kailey.
       p.   cm.
   A collection of fiction, creative nonfiction, and poetry from 33 of Colorado's gay,
lesbian, bisexual, and transgendered writers.
   ISBN 978-1-55566-398-8
   1. Gays' writings, American—Colorado. 2. Bisexuals' writings, American—Colorado. 3.
Transsexuals' writings, American—Colorado. 4. Gays—Literary collections. 5. Gay men—
Literary collections. 6. Lesbians—Literary collections. 7. Bisexuals—Literary collections. 8.
Transsexuals—Literary collections. I. Kailey, Matt.
   PS508.G39F63 2007
   810.8'0920664—DC22

                        2007019305

Printed in the United States of America

FOR ELVER BARKER
1920–2004

And for all the Colorado GLBT activists,
far too numerous to list here, who have worked tirelessly—
often at great personal risk and sacrifice—
to ensure that Colorado's GLBT voices
will not be silenced.

Contents

Introduction

ROM THE UGLINESS of Amendment 2 to the beauty of the Rocky Mountains, Colorado is a portrait of polarity. But what a magnificent portrait it is. We have it all—mountains and prairie, natural wonders and urban landscapes, wildlife and nightlife, with plenty of space and time for both politics and play.

Outsiders may see the state as a sanctuary for the sanctimonious, a conservative stronghold that strangles the spirit of anyone who steps outside of certain conventional boundaries. But Colorado's GLBT community knows better. Certainly, the state's political history is hardly a testament to queer tolerance, let alone inclusiveness. But those are only the headlines. Our real history tells a different story—as do our lives today.

The beginnings of Colorado's current GLBT movement go at least as far back as 1956, when the late activist Elver Barker became the principal founder of the Colorado chapter of the Mattachine Society in the Denver metro area. In 1959, the national Mattachine Society held its convention in the Mile High City—and by then, Barker was a leading member of the organization. Although Denver's Mattachine chapter eventually dissolved—under police pressure, according to most sources—Barker, also a gifted artist, writer, and teacher, remained a prominent gay-rights activist in Wyoming and Colorado until his death in Denver in 2004.

Thanks to Barker and the countless activists who worked with him and followed in his footsteps, Colorado is, for the most part, a welcoming state for GLBT people—a beautiful and supportive place that we can call home. And it hasn't gone unnoticed.

According to the Human Rights Campaign (www.hrc.org), the number of same-sex-partner households in Colorado increased by 385 percent between 1990 and 2000, which included the turbulent Amendment 2 years. And from 2000 to 2005, according to *Same-sex*

Couples and the Gay, Lesbian, Bisexual Population: New Estimates from the American Community Survey, a publication of the Williams Institute at the UCLA School of Law (www.law.ucla.edu/williams institute), Colorado had a 58 percent increase in identified same-sex couples, far above the 30 percent U.S. average, ranking it seventh in the nation for such an increase. The same study also ranked Colorado as seventh in the nation with regard to the percentage of the population that is GLB-identified. Whether this registers an influx of GLB singles and couples to the state or simply the coming out of the closeted is secondary to the fact that these newly identified GLB people obviously feel a measure of safety and comfort in Colorado.

Yes, there are some drawbacks (Marilyn Musgrave, Wayne Allard, James Dobson, and Focus on the Family come to mind), and, yes, there have been setbacks (the passage of Amendments 2 and 43 and the defeat of Referendum I among them), but through both the good times and the bad, Colorado's GLBT voices continue to be heard— over the city, over the prairie, and over the Rockies.

Focus on the Fabulous: Colorado GLBT Voices is the first-ever collection of short fiction, creative nonfiction, and poetry from GLBT writers throughout Colorado. Welcome to our state. We hope you like it as much as we do.

PART ONE

OUR HERITAGE

Seventy miles south of Denver on Interstate 25 sits an attractive, mid-sized city nestled in a valley between heaven and you're-going-to-hell. Colorado Springs is bordered on the west by a spectacular stretch of Rocky Mountain majesty that turns sunsets, cloud clusters, and even approaching storms into the stuff of fantasies. It's surprising that every calendar and postcard photographer in the country hasn't taken up residence here.

Pikes Peak, one of the most famous mountains in the world, each year draws thousands of visitors, who make their way—one way or another—to the very top of this popular tourist attraction. And nearby lies the Garden of the Gods, a park of awe-inspiring red sandstone formations too magnificent for mere mortals to have dreamed up or created. The natural beauty and wonder of the area, combined with a seemingly unlimited array of attractions and activities, clean and cozy commercial and residential districts, educational opportunities, a large military base, and the appeal of urban living coupled with outdoor splendor, make the Springs appear to be the ideal place to settle down and settle in.

Ah, but to the east . . .

There's another hill in Colorado Springs, much smaller than Pikes Peak, but almost equally as well known. And on top of this hill sits a castle—well, maybe not a castle, exactly, but certainly a modern-day version of such. Focus on the Family takes up 49 acres of otherwise useful land, accommodates approximately 1,300 staff, and greets an estimated 250,000 visitors a year, making it at least as trendy a tourist spot as Pikes Peak. Left to its own devices, Focus could be pretty much just another ultraconservative Christian conglomerate that the more moderate tend to give a wide berth. But because of the far-reaching leverage of its founder, Dr. James Dobson, Focus on the Family has become the hub of anti-gay activism in the United States and beyond, helping to earn Colorado the unofficial—and undeserved—nickname of "the Hate State" among many nonresident GLBT activists.

From Amendment 2, which was passed by Colorado voters in 1992 and would have prevented any government entity from adding sexual orientation to its nondiscrimination policies had it not been overturned by the U.S. Supreme Court, to Amendment 43, which was passed by

Colorado voters in 2006 and wrote discrimination into the state constitution with indelible ink by prohibiting same-sex marriage, Focus on the Family has insinuated itself into every crusade for GLBT inequality. With a scope of power and influence that would be the envy of any king, Dobson and his organization have almost single-handedly created an anti-gay empire that begins—but doesn't come close to ending—on Explorer Drive in Colorado Springs. But the view from the hill is magnificent.

Since its founding in 1977 in California, Focus on the Family has shifted its focus from concern for the American family to a concentrated effort to prevent gay men and lesbian women from even tasting the American pie—let alone having a slice—which is a primary reason for Colorado's conservative, anti-gay reputation. But in reality, the organization's birth date and the fact that it didn't even arrive in Colorado until the early 1990s make it a mere infant when compared with Colorado's GLBT community—almost a reaction to, rather than an impetus for, the state's progressive GLBT movement. The roots of Colorado's queer community run deep—and some of the deepest run right through the soil of Ground Zero—yup, that's Colorado Springs.

Two Militants Who Just Wouldn't Shut Up

DONACIANO MARTINEZ

*Since 1964, **Donaciano Martinez** has been a volunteer activist for several nonprofit causes in Colorado. In the early 1970s, he was among 20 people arrested and jailed during a Colorado Springs protest in support of Cesar Chavez and the Mexican farmworkers. For his many years of activism, Martinez received the 1998 Equality Award, 1999 Founders Award, 2000 Paul Hunter Award, 2001 Community Activist Award, and 2005 Movement Veterans Award. In 2006, he was among several people chosen for the Champions of Health Award for cofounding the Colorado Springs Free Clinic in 1971. La Gente Unida, a nonprofit cofounded by Martinez, received the 2002 Civil Rights Award.*

Martinez is the author of a nonprofit family history book, Martinez Fernandez Gomez 200-Year History 1780–on, *based on 15 years of his research of his ancestry in New Mexico and Colorado. The book has been at several institutions, including the Colorado History Museum, New Mexico History Museum, Chicano Humanities and Arts Council, Mexican American Library, Utah Family History Library, and Denver Public Library, for many years and was also preserved on microfilm, which remains accessible to people in all states. In addition, Martinez has authored numerous articles in Chicano, Latino, and GLBT publications over the past 40 years.*

*L*ONG BEFORE I WAS AWARE of the societal hatred of gays, I learned all too well about ethnic hatred. In search of a better life, my family was part of a big migration of Mexican Americans (Chicanos) who moved from northwestern New Mexico to Colorado Springs in the 1940s. Seeking to escape rural poverty in New Mexico, many Chicano families looked forward to an improved status in Colorado Springs. The labor of the newly arrived Chicanos was used to build Camp Carson, the Colorado Springs army post now known as Fort Carson.

But instead of reaching the land of milk and honey, my family and others ran into a wall of racism. Newspaper ads and signs in public places often had phrases like "No Mexicans or Dogs Allowed" or "Help Wanted. No Mexicans Need Apply." Even if the signs were not posted, the Mexican-hating attitude was in the air. I learned at an early age that it was not okay to be of Mexican American heritage.

That ethnic hatred was often internalized by our people, and the self-hatred expressed itself in the form of trying to alter our cultural identity. Chicanos often changed or Anglicized their names. Others claimed to be Italian, Spanish, or Greek. Many tried to hide their accents, and others lightened their dark hair to red or blonde. This type of internalized self-hatred has had a similar effect in the gay and lesbian community, leading many to conceal their true identities.

Despite assimilation attempts and ethnic intimidation, many of our people proudly retained our heritage (language, customs, religion, music, dances) within the borders of the Chicano district, which displayed vitality as it thrived and survived. The Chicano district of Colorado Springs continued to exist up until the mid-1960s, when it was broken up by the federal urban renewal program.

It is noteworthy that Chicanos in Colorado Springs never protested the injustices of the 1940s and 1950s. Perhaps it was our Catholic faith that kept us floating around, year after year, in a sea of racism as if it were somehow normal. It was not until the mid-1960s that Chicanos began to rebel.

At an early age, I knew that I was a joto (gay). I had an intense attraction to other boys and used to enjoy sneaking my grandmother's dresses from the clothesline and playfully wearing them in front of my cousins. With no interest in sports or other usual boy activities, I loved dancing and was even in ballet for two years. When we were both about age 10, a neighborhood boy and I began a steady fling that went on for a few years. Acutely aware of the hatred toward gays, we carefully masqueraded our affair while at school and in the neighborhood.

It was not until I was 15 that I was introduced to the gay subculture, which was underground back then in Colorado Springs. There were no bars or coffee shops for us. We gathered in the men's bathrooms of movie theaters, in the bushes of Acacia Park late at night, and in private homes with curtains closed. Just as I learned at an early age that it was not okay to be Chicano, I also learned that it was not okay to be gay. Just as Chicanos did not rebel against injustices, gays did not rebel against the societal hatred that kept us underground.

My activism began in the mid-1960s with the peace movement and later expanded to the Chicano and anti-poverty movements. Even within those leftist movements that boasted of being an alternative to mainstream society, the notion of gay rights got a cold reception. Many of us who were gay became disillusioned at trying to get straight leftists to include gay rights in the broader struggle for peace and justice.

That's why many people in leftist causes and in the gay community were surprised when the Gay Liberation Front (GLF) got its start in town a few months after the notorious Stonewall riots in New York in 1969. Truman Harris, Gene Shinn, Patrick Tracey, and I knew that it was bold and risky for the GLF to emerge in the midst of the right-wing mindset that was so pervasive in the city, but as experienced activists who had cut our teeth on the peace movement and in other areas, we were ready for the challenge.

Shunning the bathrooms and park bushes that had been, until then, the gay men's reality, the GLF came on the scene proud and strong with leaflets displaying the words: "Do you think gays are revolting? You bet your sweet ass we are." The GLF issued a 13-point platform of our goals and beliefs that called for an end to self-hatred and the right to determine our destiny. With photocopiers not yet easily accessible, GLF leaflets and other documents were typed on master stencil sheets that were subsequently fastened to a round drum for reproduction on an old-fashioned mimeograph machine. And shortly after we began, several gays began to drift our way.

But we were not activists with a single-issue agenda. We saw gay liberation as only one part of a broader picture that included the struggle for peace and justice by people of all oppressed groups throughout the world. Because of that fundamental belief, it was no coincidence that the GLF platform had as one of its planks the endorsement of numerous other liberation movements. Although we recognized that it was unrealistic for us to be directly involved in each and every movement for liberation, we thought it was important to express solidarity with others working for peace and justice in their respective communities.

As cofounders of the Colorado Springs GLF, we never tried to dodge the "radical" term that others often attached to our activism. In fact, we were proud to be radicals. Being radical was not about being extremist, nor was it about being violent. As radicals, we were not interested in addressing the symptoms or surface area of societal problems—we wanted to address the root.

At the apartments of various GLF activists, we held weekly discussion groups on a variety of topics designed to raise consciousness. We also set up a speakers' bureau to provide public educational forums. At our first forum, there was a good turnout of people active in the Black, Chicano, Peace, and Women's Movements. The GLF conducted the first of what would later become several presentations to classes at Colorado College (CC), and several CC students began to get involved with the group. In 1971, the CC student government voted to charter the GLF as an official campus group, but CC president Lloyd Worner vetoed the matter and was quoted in the media as saying that GLF activities "represent a threat to the institution's continued existence as a congenial place for learning." Worner noted that homosexuality was a crime under Colorado law and that any official approval of the GLF would be an endorsement of criminal behavior. The longtime Colorado law to which he referred was repealed by the state legislature the following year.

After getting our eviction notice from the CC president, the GLF kept moving forward. In late 1971, our GLF chapter joined other GLF groups in Colorado to become the first-ever gay and lesbian contingent to march in Denver with thousands of other people against the U.S. war in Vietnam. Thousands of protesters poured into the streets of Denver that day. Many straight activists commented that our gay and lesbian contingent was the liveliest and most vocal of all the groups at the event. As we marched and proudly displayed our banners, some of our loud chants included "Out of the Closets and Into the Streets" and "Two, Four, Six, Eight, Being Gay Is Just as Good as Straight." While at a gay party in Denver that night, some closeted gay men commented that they had quietly watched the antiwar protest from the sidelines and marveled at the courage it took for gays and lesbians to be so open at the peace march.

Along with marching in the streets, the Colorado Springs GLF continued the weekly discussion groups and began holding press conferences regarding gay-related injustices. With our increasing media coverage, numerous closeted and conservative men at the gay bar began to say that the GLF was going to cause the wrath of straight society to come down heavily on the heads of all gays and lesbians. As GLF activists, we countered such criticism by noting that our public actions would eventually result in gays and lesbians being able to have full and open lives without fear of discovery. Even some GLF moderates perceived the GLF as becoming too militant and sought to purge the radicals. The moderates sought to convert the GLF into a social club complete with cookie sales and picnics.

Faced with mounting pressures from without and within, the Colorado Springs GLF dissolved in early 1973. That same year, closeted men at the gay bar and moderates from the defunct GLF once again ducked for cover when Truman and I held a press conference to blast the national media for its sensational coverage of a Texas mass-murder case in which the accused killer was gay. Perhaps because of the sensitive topic and our bold denunciations, that particular press conference caused a furor that was talked about for months. As GLF cofounders, Truman and I became known as the "two militants who just wouldn't shut up."

Now we are elderly, and when we look at all the changes that have taken place over the years, Truman and I chuckle about our reputation as militants decades ago. But the fight is not yet over—and until it is, we're still speaking out for peace and justice.

• • •

Colorado Springs has been dubbed Ground Zero by a number of people for a number of reasons, including its reputation as the center of the current Evangelical Christian movement. But the city truly was Ground Zero for Colorado's GLBT community in the 1992 gay-and-lesbian-rights battle resulting from Amendment 2, a proposed amendment to the state's constitution that originated in the Springs. The amendment would have made it illegal for any government entity in Colorado to provide basic discrimination protection to gay men and lesbians and would have invalidated any protections already in existence.

The confusingly worded amendment did, in fact, pass by a slim margin, but even some voters were unsure of how to vote. A majority of "no" votes would have sunk the amendment, and some who voted "yes" claimed later to believe that they were voting in favor of gay and lesbian rights. Those who would deny such rights might be sanctimonious, but they aren't stupid— many believed that the amendment's language was intentionally misleading.

But those who favor equal rights for all aren't stupid, either. Over 150 groups formed throughout Colorado, including Equality Colorado in Denver (now Equal Rights Colorado) and Ground Zero in Colorado Springs, as the GLBT community and its supporters mobilized to fight the amendment. The Colorado Legal Initiatives Project (CLIP, now The Center's Legal Initiatives Project), which was founded to organize a legal challenge should the amendment pass and already had its plan in place, immediately sprung into action, filing an injunction to prevent the amendment from taking effect.

Then, representing several plaintiffs—including various individuals and the cities of Denver, Boulder, and Aspen, which already had sexual orientation protections in place—CLIP filed suit in a case that would become one of the most notable GLBT legal battles in U.S. history, spanning four years, entering many courtrooms, and requiring countless hours of work from dedicated attorneys and activists. And in the end, the hard work paid off—in 1996, Amendment 2 was overturned by the U.S. Supreme Court without ever having been put into effect. But the vote— and the battle—took its toll.

Dozens of individuals, organizations, businesses, and even cities decided to boycott Colorado. Some cancelled scheduled conferences or other activities in the state. Many GLBT tourists refused, or were afraid, to travel to "the Hate State." GLBT businesses were hurt. The state had to cover the legal costs of the battle. But, even more important than any economic backlash, the collective psyche of Colorado's GLBT community was hurt when we woke up on November 4, 1992, to find that the majority of our fellow citizens did not support us as equals, deserving of protection from discrimination—just like everyone else.

But the old adage "What doesn't kill us makes us stronger" was never truer. Even in our disappointment, we saw strength and hope—the strength of our activists, who worked tirelessly to defeat the discriminatory amendment; the strength of our community, which rallied around a common goal; and the hope that justice would prevail.

And it did, in more ways than we could have imagined. The *Romer v. Evans* decision, an incredible victory in and of itself, paved the way for the U.S. Supreme Court's decision in *Lawrence v. Texas*, which eliminated sodomy laws across the country. And the *Romer* case has been cited in hundreds, if not thousands, of legal victories since, from child custody to civil unions and same-sex marriage.

Far from preventing equal rights for GLBT citizens, the passage of Amendment 2 only served to increase the power of our community. And the fight brought many of us closer together.

Love in the Hate State

FRANK LYON

*A native of the United States, **Frank Lyon** was born in the South, raised in the East, and educated in the North before settling in the West. He wrote in secret for years while trying to convince everybody that he was a classical musician, a maneuver that defies explanation. He now writes openly. He's proud to have joined Colorado's GLBT community and is currently at work on a novel.*

OUR FRIENDS CALLED US "The Jack and Maury Show." Maury was forever moving into my house and then moving out again, always making some kind of big, dramatic scene. Last time, he rented a horrible little apartment near Cheesman Park, taking his golden retriever Skye with him.

This is the boy who took his dog, to live by the park, and run with the boys, and moved out of the house that Jack built, quipped one of my wittier friends. Maury was not amused. I found it funny, maybe because it was so ridiculous to think of me being butch enough to build a house. In reality, the house seemed to be falling down around me. Routine maintenance frequently slipped my mind.

But I noticed that Maury always left several things behind, so that after he moved out he had to call me to arrange to come get them.

"You don't have to call," I was forever telling him. "Just use your key."

"No. I wouldn't want to show up *unannounced*," he'd say.

Whatever. We were living apart on Election Day 1992, when Amendment 2 was on the ballot. I left the office and stopped at my polling place to vote. Then I picked up some Chinese takeout and went home to watch the returns. The house seemed chilly, so I turned up the heat. I put on a sweater. I got a headache. The phone rang.

"Are you watching these election returns?" Maury asked me. "Amendment 2 is winning, Jack. It's *winning*."

"Big surprise," I said.

"What's the matter with you?" Maury said.

"Nothing. I don't feel well."

"I need to come by and pick up my bike tomorrow," he said. "I left it in the garage."

"Fine. Just come by. If I'm not here, use your key."

"What time should I come by?"

"Anytime, Maury. Just use your key. Do you still have your key?"

"Yes. I still have my key. Oh, my god," he said. "Look at all the people voting yes on 2. This is the McCarthy era all over again, Jack. This is a nightmare."

"Listen, I'm going to let you go," I said. "Try to stay calm."

"You don't sound good. Call me if you need me," Maury said.

"I will," I said.

"No, you won't."

"Yes, I will."

"No, you *won't*," he said. "You refuse to need me. That's why I keep leaving."

"Sweetie. Maury. I'm hanging up."

On the screen, the numbers in favor of Amendment 2 went up again. "Oh, my god," Maury said. "Next thing you know they'll reinstate the sodomy laws. They'll be coming to arrest us in our bedrooms."

"That's not going to happen," I said. "I'm hanging up now."

By then, my head was throbbing. When I went to bed, Amendment 2 was passing by a comfortable margin. For a while I tossed and turned, tormented by visions of burly police officers coming into my room with handcuffs, forcing me to commit sodomy with them just to get enough evidence to arrest me. In my dreams, I was more than happy to incriminate myself. I finally fell into a heavy, exhausted sleep.

Suddenly there was a pounding at the door. I strained to open my eyes and saw red lights flashing through the window and against the bedroom walls. I tried to get up, but my limbs felt too heavy to move. Then a policeman burst into my bedroom, hurried across the room, and tried to open the window—a window I knew I had painted shut a long time ago. When he couldn't open it, he took out his nightstick and broke the glass. As he turned toward me, I saw that he was wearing a gas mask.

They'll be coming to arrest us in our bedrooms, Maury had said. He was right. They had come for me.

"Oh, my god," I moaned. "Officer, please. No. Not the windows. I have rights."

The officer leaned over me and slapped at my cheek with one hand. "This is for your own good," he said. "Can you tell me your name?"

"My name is Jack. I have civil rights. I have *civil rights.*"

His face was very, very pale behind his mask. "Not anymore," he said. "Colorado State Sodomy Statutes as reinstated by Amendment 2. Say goodbye to your nice house, Jack."

"What? What?" I said. Then the bedroom door opened wider and two men came in with a gurney. They tried to put a plastic mask over my face. "No," I said. "Please. No. What are you doing?"

"Just breathe, Jack. Be still."

I breathed into the mask. "Jack be nimble," I said. I laughed. It seemed very funny. "Jack be quick."

"Jack," said the cop. "Can you hear me? When was the last time you had your furnace inspected, Jack?"

"I don't . . . am I supposed to have the furnace inspected?"

I didn't hear the answer.

I woke in a hospital bed surrounded by cornflower blue curtains, oxygen tubes in my nose. The bed was blessedly cool and soft. Maury was slumped in a chair beside me, asleep. His cheeks were slightly rosy and his wavy hair was uncombed.

"Maury?"

It woke him. He got up off the chair and sat on the side of my bed, caressing my face. "Don't worry. Everything's okay," he said. "You're going to be fine." He took my hand and clutched it to his chest. "Oh, my god. Don't you *ever* do that to me again."

"What exactly did I do to you?"

"You might have *died*, Jack. You got carbon monoxide poisoning from your furnace. The policeman said that when he got there you were completely incoherent."

"But why did the policeman—"

"Something seemed really wrong," Maury said. "I tried to call you again, and I couldn't get you. I drove over and pounded on the door and there was no answer. I called 911."

"You saved my life," I said.

A tear fell out of Maury's eye and rolled down his cheek. He sniffled.

"I guess you really need me, huh?" he said, a hopeful look in his eyes.

I nodded and smiled. "Yeah. I guess I really do."

He beamed. "Oh, by the way, I told the nurses in the ER that I'm your younger brother. I was afraid they wouldn't let me in here if I wasn't immediate family. Oh, my *god*, Jack. I love you so much. Please don't ever do that again." He flung his head on my chest and started to sob.

"I promise you, I won't," I said.

"Amendment 2 passed," he said through his tears. "They won."

"Sweetie." I petted his hair. "For the last few months an entire team of attorneys has been preparing for this very situation. Okay? Honey? Listen to me."

"They're trying to erase us from the face of the planet."

"Shh. Don't make things seem worse than they are. Maury, come home."

He sat up. He took a blue bandana from his back pants pocket and blew his nose in it. "What?"

"Come home," I said. I took a deep drag of oxygen. "Unless you want your independence."

"No. I don't. I want you," he said. He buried himself in my arms again. "I just want you."

We clung to one another. The curtains parted and a nurse came in, wheeling a machine to check my vital signs. She saw us there—me with the plastic tubes up my nose, Maury weeping with his head on my chest, and my hands buried in Maury's thick hair in a completely incriminating way.

"Whoops," I said, high on my oxygen, and Maury tore himself away, staring up guiltily, all drama.

"It's—um. We're very close," he said to the nurse. "We're a very close family."

I smiled at her. She smiled at me. She left us alone.

• • •

Colorado Springs held its first PrideFest celebration and parade in 1991 with a handful of participants, and since then, the event has been a yearly attraction welcoming over 10,000 people every third Sunday in July. Boulder, Fort Collins, Pueblo, Grand Junction, and several other communities throughout the state also stage annual Pride events, drawing increasingly larger crowds at each celebration. But the granddaddy of them all is Denver's PrideFest parade and festival, which takes place every year during the last weekend in June—in tribute, of course, to the historic Stonewall Inn riots in New York City, which occurred on June 28, 1969, and continued off and on for several days. Denver held its first "official" Pride celebration, a picnic in Cheesman Park, in 1975. The following year, Denver's first Pride parade took place, drawing a few hundred celebrants.

Over thirty years later, the GLBT Community Center of Colorado's PrideFest parade and festival draws over 200,000 participants and has been recognized as one of the top ten Pride events in the country, averaging 175 parade entries and 280 vendor booths. The annual event has become so popular over the years that it has expanded to two full days, with family activities and other events adding to the weekend festivities.

But the parade's the thing, and for one glorious Sunday every summer, Denver's Cheesman Park is awash in rainbow colors, floats, and costumed parade participants. The roar of motorcycles and the thump of dance music can be heard up and down Colfax Avenue as thousands line the street to watch the parade and grab for beads and other souvenirs tossed from passing floats.

Of course, there are the annual complaints—burly men in leather vests decry the media attention wrought by outlandish drag queens in high heels, high hems, and high hair, and worry that the community is being misrepresented by an eccentric few, while the drag queens remind them of just exactly who led the charge at the Stonewall Inn decades ago. Older activists fret about the young partiers who say "Stonewall what?" and forget to acknowledge the blood, sweat, and tears that brought about this colossal celebration in the first place. But nobody complains about the hot men

dancing on elaborately constructed floats or the hot women roaring by on their Harleys. Denver's PrideFest is definitely here, it's queer, and most people in the city have already gotten used to it, which is why they come out in droves to join the party.

But PrideFest means something different to everyone, and the real beauty of the event is that each person gets to experience it in his or her own way, with memories that live on long after the rainbow flags have been put away for another year and the last piece of crepe paper has been swept from the street.

Yuri: A Pride Memoir

JERRY L. WHEELER

*After 25 years in the corporate world, **Jerry L. Wheeler** dropped
out of his cubicle and began writing part-time. Previously published
in Greg Wharton and Ian Philips'* Law of Desire: Tales of Gay Male Lust
and Obsession *(Suspect Thoughts Press), as well as online in Sean
Meriwether's* Velvet Mafia, *he is hard at work on his first novel.*

J'LL CALL HIM YURI. He was short and stocky, with short
brown hair and watery aquamarine eyes. In his early thirties,
Yuri had only been out for a few furtive years in his native country. He was staying in Denver on a tourist visa with some people he'd met
online. It would be his first Pride parade.

My friend Arthur had found Yuri in a chat room and asked him out to
the Wrangler, a local leather-and-Levi's bar, for a drink the Friday of
Pride weekend. I went along to provide moral support for Arthur and an
excuse to leave if necessary.

Their eyes met, and it was magic. It was bliss. It was heaven. It was
a quick drink and then total abandonment. They hopped in a cab before my ice could melt, leaving me at the north end of the bar to be
pawed by a drunken bear with a shaved head who leered at me, fell
asleep, then woke up and leered at me again. I wasn't sure if he was
tired, drunk, or narcoleptic.

When Arthur and Yuri arrived at my Pride party the next day, they
looked as if they hadn't seen much daylight. Their eyes may have been
dull, but they only looked at each other anyway. Yuri sat on Arthur's lap
or with his back between Arthur's legs as they stretched out on the lawn
beneath the shade of the box elder in the backyard, eating from the same
plate. They were at the charged particle stage of the relationship, where

constant physical contact had to be maintained or they'd be thrown off into the dating vortex once more.

We hated them. No. We envied them. We didn't hate them until after the third pitcher of margaritas, when we started taking bets on whether the relationship would last hours or days. And even then, we *still* envied them—because they were long gone by that time, off to Arthur's apartment where Yuri was spending Pride weekend, leaving us to speculate on their future until well past midnight.

We reconvened at eight the next morning at Arthur's love nest, where he answered the intercom in the foyer of his condo building on the first ring and buzzed us in, bounding down the hall to greet us.

"This one's a keeper!" he said, pointing back at his apartment and leaping around us with the glassy-eyed glaze of too much love and too little sleep. That clarified the situation. We'd all had experience with Arthur's keepers before, kept for somewhere between a week and a month before being thrown out like overripe bananas.

Once inside, we smiled, nodded, and made nice with the doomed Yuri, treating him with good-hearted generosity, secure in our assumption that he probably wouldn't last past Wednesday. It was, after all, Pride weekend—as Yuri continually reminded us. His enthusiasm was as refreshing as it was irritating. Charming in a goofy way, he wore a snug NYPD logo T-shirt, matching ball cap, black leather shorts, and boots.

"I have uniform fetish," he explained. We smiled and nodded some more. "When do we leave?"

"In a few minutes," Arthur replied, his hands on Yuri's shoulders. "Don't worry, we won't miss anything. We just have to go two blocks."

We downed our mimosas, made last-minute bathroom trips, and moved in the general direction of the door. Yuri prodded and swept us along, his camera already out of the bag. He snapped pictures of Arthur locking the door behind us, and then he was gone, covering the two blocks by the time we had congregated on the sidewalk. We heard him calling Arthur's name, and Arthur was soon running off, too. As we got closer, we saw Yuri, posing with his arms around a group of Denver cops, his grin as toothy as a sturgeon's. Arthur manned the camera while Yuri shouted out the angles he wanted.

"From *here*! Now *here*! Try one from *this* side now."

The shoot might have gone on forever if we hadn't heard the motorcycles. The crowd buzzed and necks arched as parade watchers tried to see down the street. Yuri leapt away from the policemen with quick thanks, grabbed Arthur's arm, and disappeared into the crowd. We followed more slowly, taking time to say hello to people we knew as we worked our way toward the Colfax Avenue parade route.

Motorcycles roared as we approached the curb, and there was Yuri, giving a "thumbs up" to the camera, posing on the knee of a butch leather dyke on a Harley. Then Arthur and Yuri scurried to the sidelines, where Arthur lit a cigarette. Yuri frowned at him when he wasn't looking, pretending to check the camera.

A disco thump preceded the arrival of the twink bar float, but Yuri saw it coming first. "Look," he shouted, "they are *dancing*." And then he broke into the most arrhythmic cluster of moves a non-neuropath could possibly make, whipping his baseball cap in the air and grabbing Arthur from behind. Yuri ground his crotch deeper into Arthur's ass with each block the float progressed, until it was finally within leaping distance. He then tossed Arthur aside like Godzilla discarding a busload of tourists and advanced on the dancing twinks with his finger on the camera's shutter trigger.

They must have seen him coming. Just as he moved within focusing range, they began pelting him and the rest of the crowd with a mix of condoms and rainbow refrigerator magnets. Yuri seized upon the trinkets as if they were manna from Heaven, lowering his camera and stuffing the tiny pockets of his leather shorts. It didn't take long until they were full.

Throughout the morning, Yuri collected kitschy favors and free passes from every float and car that passed, hauling Arthur around by the waistband of his cargo shorts. He crammed Arthur's pockets so full of loot that his misshapen thighs bulged—picture Pan in flip-flops and a Cher T-shirt. And when Yuri wasn't picking up treasure, he was taking pictures of banners and political candidates stumping for votes.

"Look, look," he said excitedly, pointing at a tanned woman with graying brown hair, sixtyish but marching enthusiastically in a PFLAG T-shirt, her face polished with a thin sheen of sweat. The placard she carried read "I LOVE MY GAY SON!!!!" Yuri snapped a picture.

"I *love* my gay son!" he said. "Can you fucking believe it?"

I COULD BELIEVE IT, but apparently he couldn't. Ugly American that I am, it had taken me that long to understand that he was documenting a sentiment that he didn't see expressed regularly at home, as if to prove to himself that a place existed where you could be proud of who you were.

Yuri's enthusiasm took on a more poignant note for me after that. I saw him with admiration instead of annoyance, watching a man in the throes of becoming, of stepping out from behind whatever walls trapped him so that he could gaze at the vistas they had obstructed. I had scanned those same horizons long ago, but they were too familiar to move me anymore. Their magic had turned to monotony. Watching Yuri discover them gave them a vitality they hadn't had in years for me.

For a moment, I was nineteen and going to my first Pride parade—innocent, vulnerable, and staggered by the complexity of my newfound community. My stomach became queasy with possibilities, the way it had then, and standing right there on the corner of Colfax and Emerson in Denver, on a bright, hot morning in late June, with thousands of my fellow queers surrounding me, a tear welled up in the corner of my eye—just the way it had that day, so many years ago.

THREE HUNDRED SEVENTY-TWO pictures later, it was over. The last banner had flown and the last float had dropped its loot. Yuri stood holstering his camera amidst the parade detritus. Stray condoms dropped out of his overstuffed pockets every time he moved. Plastic bracelets were stacked like vertebrae up his arms. The Mardi Gras beads garnishing his head and shoulders clacked as he and Arthur jogged toward us.

"Did you see the parade?" he shouted. "It was so *beautiful!*"

"Of course they saw it," Arthur said, beaming at Yuri.

"What now?" Yuri asked, shifting his weight from one foot to the other like a five-year-old who needs to pee.

"I thought we'd all go back to my place for another round of mimosas, then head down to the festival," Arthur said. "Is that okay with everybody?"

We all nodded and murmured our agreement as Yuri's eyes widened.

"More? You mean there is *more?*"

"Of course. There's a whole festival with food and music and stuff."

"Just for being gay?" Yuri asked.

Arthur grinned with smitten indulgence. "I guess you could say that."

Back at Arthur's place, Yuri downloaded photos onto his laptop. He shouted and pointed at the images, reliving the last forty-five minutes as heartily as he'd spent them. He catalogued and sorted the pictures, and when he was finished, he fidgeted in Arthur's computer desk chair while we talked and drank.

Finally he sighed, went into the kitchen, and came back with a bottle of water. "When is festival?"

"Oh, it goes on all day," Arthur said. "We don't want to get there too early—it'll be easier to move around once the parade crowd thins out."

Yuri sipped and frowned as if he were swallowing more than water, a look Arthur must have noticed. "But we could start walking down there," Arthur hedged, looking at everyone else for agreement. "C'mon, drink up and let's hit the road. Anyone need the bathroom?" Even when he was in love, he was still in total control.

The reek of funnel cakes, deep-fryer grease, and warm beer hit us as we were crossing Broadway in front of a verdant drag queen—stick-thin and outfitted in green tights, green tutu *avec* spangles, bobbing antennae, magic wand, and green platform boots. Yuri grabbed her around the waist and posed with her in the middle of the intersection while Arthur snapped his brains out.

They hit the festival like a tornado gutting a trailer park, cutting a random swath of mirth and exhilaration. We were swept along breathlessly, lurching from one destination to the next until we couldn't do it anymore. We wanted some time to talk with friends, have a quiet beer, or at least sit down. We made plans to meet them by the fountain in two hours to go to lunch.

They showed up two hours and forty-three minutes later, staggering under the weight of at least ten plastic sacks full of T-shirts, brochures, flyers, and handouts. Well, Arthur was staggering anyway. Yuri looked as if he were ready to run a marathon.

"*Three* memory cards!" he shouted as he ran toward us. "Three memory cards *full*!" Clearly a personal best.

His energy was no longer infectious. We were all showing signs of Pride wear and tear—especially Arthur, who had a good ten years on Yuri.

"Are we ready for lunch?" Arthur asked wearily, dragging his bags on the ground.

Lunch threatened to be more of the same. Yuri snapped various views of us at the table, demanding smiles and poses until the waitress politely forced him to sit down and look at the menu. He wasn't even going to drink the Jägermeister shot we ordered for him until we convinced him that it was a Pride ritual. The next three shots were *his* idea.

The alcohol kept him in his chair long enough to scroll through his pictures until the food came, passing the camera around to share a few choice shots. Once he had eaten, he sank fast—into drunken gratitude.

"I say thank you to all my new American friends," he slurred as he put his arm around Arthur. "And I especially like to thank my daddy, Arthur."

Arthur choked so hard, it appeared that the Heimlich might be in order. His face reddened and his eyes bulged until he finally swallowed the word *daddy*. And the sour look on his face said he didn't much like the taste of it. Yuri was too busy hugging us to notice. A photo of them at that moment would have proven more prophetic than any taken that weekend. They broke up in less than a week.

ARTHUR SOLDIERS ON, in search of yet another keeper. Yuri moved to Canada and got married to a sugar beet farmer named Dale in Saskatchewan a month later, but that doesn't matter. I only include it because the stories I like best have endings. That weekend is all that matters. Both Arthur and Yuri will have that to savor whenever their lives get too bland.

Because Yuri's life *will* become bland. If he stays in the gay community, no matter where he is, leather dykes on motorcycles and green-sequined drag queens will become as commonplace as putting on his shoes or brushing his teeth. And even though all the fanfare is *not* just for being gay—even though it's about history and civil rights and struggle and oppression and celebrating the escape from our collective closet—he'll find that freedom breeds complacency, even though it shouldn't. And when that happens, I hope he finds a way to fill his eyes with wonder once again.

We should all be so lucky.

• • •

Partly in spite of, and partly because of, the overly conservative segment of Colorado's population, the state's activists have remained hard at work and have continued to make history.

With the passage of Amendment 2, many GLBT Coloradans came out—literally—to fight the good fight. And as the GLBT community continues to move away from the closet and toward visibility and activism, attitudes, policies—and even laws—are changing.

Although Colorado governor Roy Romer was forced to uphold the voice of the voters during the Amendment 2 legal battle, he did not personally favor the amendment and was considered an ally of the GLBT community. Other straight politicians have become outspoken advocates for the community, including Denver mayors Federico Peña, Wellington Webb, and John Hickenlooper. Mayor Webb formed the first Gay and Lesbian Advisory Committee to the mayor's office, which was continued and enhanced by Mayor Hickenlooper and is now the mayor's GLBT Commission. Both Mayor Webb and Mayor Hickenlooper have appointed openly gay and lesbian staff and have marched in Denver's PrideFest parade.

Straight politicians in many areas of the state, including Colorado Springs, make their presence known at various GLBT events and actively court the GLBT vote. Openly gay and lesbian candidates run for, and are elected to, city and state offices, including the Colorado legislature. In 2007, two transsexual candidates announced their bids for city offices. And several Colorado cities now include both sexual orientation and "gender variance" in their nondiscrimination policies.

The GLBT community is definitely alive and well in Colorado. In fact, it has never been more alive or healthier, despite what might appear to be another setback. In November 2006, Colorado again made history when it became the first state ever to offer both a domestic partnership initiative and an anti-same-sex-marriage amendment on the same ballot in the general election. Hopes were high for Referendum I, which was sponsored in the state house and senate by two straight legislators. Money poured in and volunteers poured out into the streets to garner support for the measure, which would have provided a host of legal protections to same-sex couples.

But even as activists were developing a cautious optimism about the possibility of the measure passing, no one could ignore the rumblings of opposition from the south. There was little question that Amendment 43, the anti-same-sex-marriage amendment born in Colorado Springs, would garner enough signatures to appear on the ballot, but the two measures were not in opposition, so voters could actually support or reject them both if they so chose. But even as some of those who argued in favor of Amendment 43 and the sanctity of marriage were violating the sanctity of their own, the amendment passed, the domestic partnership referendum failed (by a relatively small margin), and GLBT Coloradans again woke up after election day to wonder why the majority of our fellow citizens did not support us as equals, deserving of protection from discrimination—just like everyone else.

But once again, the community saw activists working around the clock, various factions of the community coming together for a common cause, and straight allies stepping in to help. Just as other setbacks have not deterred the Colorado queer community, neither will this one. The community just keeps getting bigger, stronger, better—and more beautiful. After all, how many states can boast that they are home to the first drag queen ever to appear in *Forbes* magazine? Only one. That's right—Colorado.

My Vespa Scooter Theft Adventure or Why You Should Never, Ever Steal from a Drag Queen

Nuclia Waste

Nuclia Waste, the triple-nippled drag queen of comedy, has been delighting audiences in Colorado, the United States, Canada, and Mexico with her wacky stand-up comedy wit and rule-breaking fashion sense. She writes the bimonthly column "City Seen" for Out Front Colorado *newspaper in Denver. From comedy shows to charity fundraisers, the Princess of Plutonium radiates her joy and belief that you should never take life too seriously. She is the most original entertainer to ever emerge from the uranium-contaminated swamps of Rocky Flats, Colorado. Having three breasts has not hurt her career, either. Oh, the joys and benefits of nuclear radiation!*

Nuclia and her green Vespa scooter were featured in the April 2005 issue of Forbes, *making her the first drag queen ever to appear in the financial magazine. The theft of Nuclia's green Vespa made national news when she was quoted on the Perspective page of* Newsweek. *For more info about Nuclia Waste, visit www.NucliaWaste.com.*

*I*T WAS A DARK AND STORMY NIGHT. Okay. Not really. It was another fabulous sunny Saturday in Colorado, and the plan for Mr. Waste and me that Fourth of July weekend was camping high in the Colorado Rocky Mountains—the kind of camping that's done in a tent, not in platform go-go boots, though both are quite fun. As the Triple Nipple Drag Queen of Comedy, I should know.

That evening, while we were roasting marshmallows for s'mores over an open fire, my fluorescent green Vespa scooter with the hot pink flames was having a weekend vacation of its own back in Denver, zooming down Colfax Avenue without me. This is the same scooter that I straddled in the April 2005 issue of *Forbes* magazine, making me the first drag queen ever to appear in *Forbes*, and making my scooter so infamous that my friend Michele instantly recognized the Vespa when she saw it—but not the rider, who was lacking big green hair and three boobs. (I live in the Plutonium Palace in Rocky Flats, Colorado, and the radiation blesses me in many unique ways.)

Michele fired off an e-mail to alert me, but to no avail. I was still frolicking in the wilderness, putting on a show for the gay motorcycle club, The Rocky Mountaineers. Upon returning home Sunday morning, Mr. Waste and I discovered our garage door wide open and my *Forbes*-famous scooter gone! The police were called, forms were filled out, and a neighbor came forth to say that some kids were seen in the alley on Saturday afternoon. But knowing that the police were never going to make a stolen scooter a top priority, even if it did belong to the Princess of Plutonium, I decided that it was time to shift into Nancy Drew mode and take matters into my own opera-length-gloved hands.

Putting on my best Angela-Lansbury-*Murder-She-Wrote* wig, I deduced:

1. If the kids seen in the alley arrived on foot, they might live nearby.

2. Being kids, they might have stolen the Vespa for a joy ride.

3. Being kids, they're probably not yet reading *Forbes* and don't realize this is possibly the most famous scooter in the country. My custom-green Day-Glo paint job can be seen for miles.

4. Since that Sunday was another beautiful, sunny Colorado day, they might be riding it right at that moment.

Time to take action. The thieves didn't know it, but I keep a backup scooter, like Batgirl, and soon I was one pissed-off drag queen with some very fast wheels, riding around the neighborhoods of Denver looking for the perpetrators. Denver's no Gotham City, but this superhero was gonna fight tooth and Lee Press-On Nail to solve the crime.

Faster than you can say "Holy Atomic Scooter," I spied my Vespa within minutes of my house. The scooter was still green, and I was very red. Two kids were on board having the time of their lives. Like the Batmobile, my scooter screeched to a halt in front of them, cutting off their escape.

"Get off that bike, park it, and turn off the engine. You are riding a stolen bike and I am calling the police." I was talking so butch, I'm sure I was channeling Cagney *and* Lacey.

Trembling on my scooter were a 16-year-old boy and his 10-year-old younger brother. The little one made off like the Joker, but his older brother stayed put. He was either in shock or taking too many drugs to care. I called 911 and we waited for the police. The whole time I was wondering when this kid was going to bolt, too. What I wouldn't have given for Wonder Woman's lariat of truth right then. But he stayed put. Must have been some good drugs.

While waiting the usual eternity for the men in blue, I chatted the kid up. He got the scooter "from a friend," he told me, and he thought it might be stolen. He was out on bail, released from jail just a few days earlier. Who needs a lariat of truth when your criminal is spilling his guts like that? Then he asked if he could use my cell phone to call his mom.

"Okay," I said. "Hmmm, let's see. You probably stole my scooter. It's been stripped, trashed, wrecked and defaced, almost beyond recognition. And now you want to use the minutes on my cell phone. That would be a big . . . NO!"

The police finally arrived. Our criminal had no ID and gave a fake name to the officers. Even I knew better than to tell the police that my name is Nuclia Waste. So the perpetrator was put in handcuffs until they could sort out the real story.

After verifying the VIN number and confirming that the scooter matched the stolen vehicle report I filed earlier that day, the police arrested the kid and it was off to the big house.

Sadly, my poor scooter had to be put down (play taps here). I have never loved anything so much that vibrated between my legs. Luckily, my auto insurance came through with enough money to fund my next scooter project, The Atomic Blast. It's bigger, faster, greener, and more radioactive than ever. It's the world's first glow-in-the-dark scooter, coming to a crime-fighting town near you.

Just like a Nancy Drew novel, my stolen scooter story does have a happy ending—and a moral: Never, ever steal from a drag queen. She will hunt you down and make you pay. And she'll look fabulous the whole time she's doing it.

• • •

From Focus to PrideFest and from Dobson to drag queens, Colorado really does have it all—even if we don't necessarily want it all. But that's just one of the many features that make the state so interesting. Those who love Colorado really love it—even if they stray, they usually find their way back, again and again. Because Colorado is more than politics, as important, rewarding, and life changing as those political battles can be. For most of us—the conservative and the liberal, the Evangelical and the atheist, the homophobic preacher and the radical queer—Colorado is home.

Part Two

Our Home

Years ago, the residents of Colorado started a little civil war, pitting those born and bred in the state against those who moved to Colorado from somewhere else, ostensibly just to annoy the natives. Bumper stickers resembling the Colorado license plate at the time—green mountains set against a white sky—took up residence on many a car, proclaiming "Native" or "Transplant," with an invisible field of superiority surrounding the natives' jeeps or SUVs. A Colorado birth certificate was a badge of honor so coveted that it's surprising that the natives didn't simply glue *those* onto their bumpers in place of a sticker and then drive around town to show them off to the transplanted rabble who arrived just a little too late to be real Coloradans, but who also wanted a place to call home.

Colorado can do that to a person. There is something about the state that draws people in and doesn't let them go, that makes them possessive and protective, and that causes even non-natives to grouse about the newly relocated, redefining "transplant" as anyone who moved here after they did. The pull of Colorado is strong for many people—strong enough that John Denver wrote about it in "Rocky Mountain High," and millions of people understood exactly what he was talking about. Even those who have never been here before often finally find their "home" when they arrive.

Most people can relate to the concept of home—of having a place to put down their roots and put up their feet, a place of comfort, security, and unconditional acceptance. Home is sometimes a more difficult notion for GLBT people, because we have often felt, or have actually been, displaced—kicked out of our own houses or family situations, fired from jobs, harassed by neighbors, physically threatened, or even physically attacked. The safety that "home" provides is sometimes lacking in our lives. When laws don't protect, when neighborhoods reject, and when welcome seems far away, it can be that much harder to develop a sense of place—a feeling of acceptance, belonging, and identification with a geographical area, whether it be a country, state, city, or block.

Colorado has provided this sense of place for many members of the GLBT population. Queer culture flourishes here, with films, theatre, museum exhibits, art gallery showings, cabaret, and music festivals that cater to and reflect GLBT talent and interests. And with the abundance of businesses, organizations, activities, and support and social groups that are GLBT-owned, GLBT-friendly, or that have been established specifically for the GLBT community, we know where we belong.

But Colorado queer culture is not the only draw. The land itself speaks to those who enjoy the beauty of the mountains, the clean, crisp air, the amazing night sky when devoid of city lights, the proliferation of wildflowers in the summer, and the golden leaves of the aspen in the fall. Perhaps the land speaks to GLBT people most of all—our long-ago history reflects a deep connection with nature. Among many indigenous populations throughout the world, GLBT people were, and occasionally still are, seen as healers and shamans, people with a special relationship to the gods and to the earth. It would make sense, then, that we would have some attachment, even as Western culture has paved over the natural world, cementing society's disengagement with the land and the place of human beings within the scheme of things.

Colorado offers up its natural wonders to everyone, and for GLBT people, it is often not just where we find our home, but where we find ourselves.

For Mission Columbia

BARRY JAY GLASS

Barry Glass's writing career has been long and varied. The first story he remembers writing is now encased in a time capsule within the cornerstone of his elementary school gymnasium, a place he otherwise avoided like kryptonite.

In the 1980s and '90s, Barry wrote an op-ed column, "The Glass Eye," for Resolute, *the newsletter of the People with AIDS Coalition of Colorado. In 1983, he began his work as a social worker with HIV-positive gay men and their caregivers. These early experiences continue to inform his work and his life. During that time, Barry chronicled the first ten years of the Denver AIDS epidemic. A serialized form of his work appeared in* Resolute *alongside personal stories of those he came to know and love. Barry was also the executive director of Bearing Witness, a nonprofit organization focused on the exhibition of HIV/AIDS-inspired art, writing, and culture.*

Barry loves to write, yet remains undisciplined. At year's end, he always vows to do better. He considers his acceptance into this anthology as encouragement and appreciates the opportunity to be part of this important project.

WHEN I WAS GROWING UP in New York City, there was a movie theatre called the Loew's Paradise. It sat in the middle of the Grand Concourse in the Bronx, and although I can't remember much about the movies I saw there, I don't have to close my eyes to remember the ceiling. It was a high enchanted dome, sprinkled with stars of varying size and intensity. If I leaned back in my chair and stared at the ceiling, I believed that I was up there, far away and flying through space.

In school, my favorite field trips were those we took to the Planetarium, where I lost myself in a three-dimensional never-ending journey across the universe. In second grade, I entered a school writing contest with a short story about my adventures in space and the arrival of a friendly Martian here on Earth. I was chosen as one of the winners, and my entry was placed in a time capsule scheduled for opening in 2008. At the time, I hoped that when I got to read my story again, fifty years down the line, my imagined solar system would be more fact than fiction, and that spaceship travel, like the automobile, would be a way of life.

An avid reader, I had the full set of Tom Swift space adventure books alongside my prized Hardy Boy collection. A mobile of the solar system hung from the ceiling of my bedroom, and without looking, I could recite the names of the nine planets in order of their distances from the sun. I was partial to the beauty of Saturn's rings and the loneliness of distant Pluto.

Yet I didn't grow up to become an astronomer or an astronaut. My mother's warnings about being realistic kept my feet on the ground. But I never stopped looking up.

In 1971, I took my first trip west of the Mississippi and came to Denver to visit some friends who had recently moved here. Two of us took a car trip to Los Angeles by way of Las Vegas, drove up the California coast to San Francisco, and returned to Colorado through Utah. As a city boy raised in skyscraper canyons, I was awed by the panoramic vistas and pledged an everlasting love to the western highway.

We traveled from one unforgettable moment to another and wound our way homeward. One August midnight, we camped near the summit of Independence Pass, ten miles outside of Aspen. After dinner, lying in a sleeping bag and looking at the sky, I was transported through time to a cherished afternoon spent under the dome of the Loew's Paradise. Only then, the stars were never within reach. But that summer evening, when there was no voice insisting that I lower my head and watch the movie, I stayed awake and caught up with myself in space.

• • •

The mountains of Colorado embody the power, spirit, and magnificence of the state. Many people are drawn to them time and time again, not only for the skiing, snowboarding, hiking, snowshoeing, backpacking, and other sporting adventures that they offer, but for the scenic beauty of snow-capped peaks, the mountain meadows filled with flowers, and the wildlife—from marmots to mountain goats and deer to bighorn sheep—that can cross the road at just the right time, turning a casual drive into a wilderness adventure.

The mountains can even be seen as a metaphor for Colorado's GLBT community—steadfast, strong, and standing proud in the face of adversity, which for the mountains can mean logging, mining, drilling, forest fires, and attempts to privatize wilderness areas for corporate gain, and for us can mean anti-gay laws, policies, and legal battles. But the mountains were here long before their adversaries and will remain long after those who seek to harm them are gone—much like our community. We're not going anywhere.

But there's another part of Colorado that is equally awe-inspiring and equally enduring—the vast open spaces that contain farmland and prairie and that hold a beauty of their own that tourists often miss. Those of us who are attached to the land and who live on it, and with it, every day have integrated it into our lives until it becomes a part of us—as natural to us as who we love and who we are.

Wild Prairie Sage

SUZANNE MARIE CALVIN

Suzanne Marie Calvin has been published in various venues, from freelance articles for Moms Online/Oxygen Media *to the three novels she has published both in e-book format and print copies. Suzanne lives on the Colorado prairie with her partner of three years, their two children, eighteen horses, five chickens, three cats, one dog . . . and a wild prairie grouse in a tumbleweed tree. She is currently working on several projects, one of which is a lesbian romance novel based on Devon and Sophie, the characters in this anthology short. Visit her Web site at www.SuzanneMarieCalvin.com or contact her at writer4romance@pcisys.net.*

SOPHIE ALWAYS SAID that Devon had rescued her.

Shuffling into the kitchen, idly retrieving a glass of water, Devon didn't feel heroic. Disgruntled, mostly with herself, she watched Sophie out of the corner of her eye, pretending to ignore her because of their most recent fight. Their conflicts were tears in the fabric of their relationship—tiny slits, or big ones, depending on the magnitude of the argument. Making up was always like darning socks, one careful stitch at a time, with a little tug at each suture to make sure it would hold.

At the kitchen table, Sophie was bundling sage that grew wild on the eastern Colorado prairie. After their heated exchange that morning, she'd kicked on a pair of old jeans and shoved infuriated fists through the arms of her tank top. Tugging a baseball cap over her short hair, which was still mussed beyond sexy from sleep, she had then tromped out of the house in flip-flops Devon thought had no business being on the prairie. There were cactus and prairie-dog holes and snakes out there, for chrissake. Nevertheless, Sophie—pure Venus and attitude—had jabbed her nose at the air, resolve in every step she took toward her destination.

Beautiful breasts, unchained, nodded under her top. The round behind Devon loved to grab at least a hundred times a day swung with each step. Arms cut through the air by her sides, fists punching with each stride as she marched across the yellow, summer-parched prairie grass. Barely pausing at their fence line, she swung a long, denim-clad leg over the barbed wire, losing a flip-flop in the process. In spite of her own anger and frustration, Devon found herself muffling a chuckle as she watched Sophie scramble to slap it back on her foot.

With a visible huff, Sophie made a beeline for the lush, bushy spots where wild prairie sage grew best. She'd been eyeing it for weeks, muttering quietly each time they walked the pasture that she needed to "get out there and harvest some" for bundling.

Devon wished she could stop watching her partner. On some level, it felt like she was breaching their argument-induced vow of silence. Clenching a toothpick between her teeth, she noted that Sophie hadn't looked back even once—she must have known Devon was staring.

Flustered, Devon decided two could play that game. A vow of silence was a vow of silence. It involved ignoring each other, pretending to get on with the day even if their minds were still wrapped around the heated discussion of earlier. So Devon had spent the morning out with the horses, trying to forget all of the angry, stupid things she'd said, which had incited angry, stupid words from Sophie.

Yet Sophie always said that Devon had rescued her.

Devon didn't want that much credit. It was true that she had helped Sophie leave the bastard she'd been married to for twenty years, but with more integrity than Devon might have managed if the tables were turned, Sophie walked away from the marriage with little more than severely battered self-esteem, two suitcases, and two amazing kids who spent the weekends with their biological father.

The toothpick snapped in Devon's mouth and she realized frustration had locked her jaw. Sophie's ex was the warning gunshot for most of their disagreements, which seemed to take off like a bullet at the starting gate before ultimately fizzling out once they both simmered down and managed civility again.

With every action and every word, the man infuriated Devon, while Sophie was focused on moving on with her life, which included trying to forget that her ex even existed. And once Devon's irritation lifted, she would realize that, after twenty years, Sophie needed the freedom associated with not having to discuss her ex. Freedom from abuse. Freedom from despair, emotional obliteration, and the near-death of her incredible spirit.

Freedom to sit for hours bundling wild sage.

Devon had spent her life establishing a career and drifting in and out of committed relationships. After surviving breast cancer, she lived six years alone, a time she fondly referred to as a "journey to herself." When she had moseyed into Sophie's life, a "gentle, Zen-sustained rancher with a new lease on living," as Sophie described her, Devon was ready to settle down with a lifemate. And Sophie was more than ready to leave her husband. She called Devon her "knight in shining armor."

It was a pretentious, dreamy-eyed description for what Devon had done, which had literally consisted of tossing Sophie, her two children, and their suitcases into her pickup, then whisking them off to live with her on the ranch.

Perhaps to Sophie, who had grown so much in such a short time, Devon's actions may have seemed heroic in the moment. The irony was that Devon thought of Sophie as the brave one. Sophie, who had spent the last few years, maybe longer, finding herself and then finding the courage to make that bold statement of who she was—first by leaving a marriage that probably never should have taken place, then by letting herself fall in love with Devon.

Now Devon watched her at their kitchen dinette, sorting through sage, making small piles that she would then bind with purple string. They used it for "smudging."

"It clears the air of everything from evil spirits to the leftover garlic from last night's pasta," Sophie had said when she first smudged the house. "It can even take tension out of the room."

Tension, Devon mused. *Like the tension created when they argued.*

She cleared her throat and contemplated breaking the silence, but saw Sophie's shoulders stiffen at the gritty sound that sliced the air. Swallowing whatever silly comment she might have attempted to make to alleviate the hostility in the room, Devon busied herself rummaging through cupboards, looking for nothing really, but looking with great zest.

Sophie lifted a fistful of sage to her nose and breathed, inhaling the rich sensual fragrance. Devon studied her discreetly from a semi-hunched position at an opened cupboard.

God, she loved this woman. And she adored Sophie's kids. She supported them emotionally and financially. They were a family, notwithstanding what the rest of the free world thought.

For the most part, their relationship was pure bliss.

Until the occasional gunshot was fired.

That morning, their quarrel had been about the ex's propensity to push boundaries. Barring child visitation exchanges and emergencies, Sophie had explicitly asked him to leave her alone. Her requests consistently went unheeded.

He couldn't even handle the simplest of tasks, like determining the length of time it took to boil pasta. Devon would have bought him a hundred cookbooks if she had thought he was truly concerned about ruining a spaghetti dinner. But it wasn't about pasta. It was about control.

"Don't you think he's driving me crazy?" Sophie had screamed that morning. "Don't you think that every time he pops back into my life, I just want to throw myself off the roof? The last thing I want is to have him calling here all of the time!"

Blinded by frustration, Devon had not understood. Now, Sophie's shrieks rang through her ears and yanked sharply at her chest.

"Imagine how you'd feel if your cancer kept coming back, no matter what you did to make it stop?" Tears had pooled in Sophie's eyes and dropped, weaving small, moist paths down her cheeks. Then, in a shaky whisper, she had said, "He's a cancer and he keeps coming back. No matter what I do."

"Stupid . . ." Devon mumbled when she thought back to that moment. It all made sense to her now. Of course she would be frustrated by a situation that she felt powerless to stop. The cancer. Sophie's ex. *How dare she let them take away her sense of control.*

But that was stupid. She could see that now. She didn't need to control the universe. She didn't even need to control Sophie's ex. She did, however, fiercely cling to the need to have control over her own life. *Didn't everyone?* And she would fight, tooth and nail, for the right she and Sophie had to love each other. For their right to make promises to each other. To be happy together.

She leaned against the counter, arms crossed over her chest.

And then there was Sophie, at the table, bundling sage in silence. The tension had left her shoulders and she actually looked quite peaceful. Even oblivious. But Devon knew that she was clinging to a tightrope with both hands, dangling over the net-less ground below. They both were.

She smiled. There was a poetic freedom in that somehow—if only the freedom of knowing they could choose to walk that tightrope together.

Freedom—to sit for hours bundling wild sage.

Devon looked away a moment and swallowed hard. Then she shuffled to the table and warily dragged a chair from where it was tucked in like the others. With cautious eyes, she watched Sophie's reaction, smiling again when her partner didn't even stop to glance up, but instead focused every ounce of her attention on tying the world's tiniest purple-stringed knot on a bundle of sage.

"You're doing a great job," Devon managed, her voice scratchy from hours of sworn silence.

"Thanks." Sophie didn't look up. Suddenly tying that knot seemed more important than life itself.

Devon cleared her throat. "I love you, you know."

Sophie swallowed hard. Then, the knot momentarily forgotten, she looked up at Devon with moist eyes and replied, "I know." Her lips wavered and a single tear escaped to glide down her cheek. "I love you, too, Devon."

Devon smiled and reached out with a tentative hand to wipe away the tear with her thumb. Sophie's lips curved into a quiet smile that sent a wave of need and longing through Devon, as dependable as the sunrise, as surprising as love at first sight.

Their love was like wild prairie sage. Fragrant. Alive. Lush and filled with everything life had to offer, renewing itself time and again each season—bolder, stronger, and more beautiful than before.

Devon picked up a handful of sage and a tiny purple string. And, in a settled, almost exhilarating silence, they tied knots together.

• • •

Many on the coasts tend to lump Colorado in with the Midwest, with visions of cowboys and cowgirls riding the open range, roping calves, and taming bucking broncos. Some areas of the state relish this image and do their best to reinforce it with wonderful Old West images of ghost towns, aging cemeteries, historic landmark preservation, and history museums. Some of the larger cities, such as Denver, have attempted to move away from a "cow town" reputation and toward an image of sophisticated urban chic.

But there are plenty of GLBT folks in all parts of Colorado who enjoy country-western music, two-stepping, line dancing, and a good old-fashioned rodeo. The Colorado Gay Rodeo Association (CGRA) provides a taste of the Wild, Wild West every year with the Rocky Mountain Regional Rodeo, which celebrated its 25th anniversary in 2007, and attendance numbers reflect the community's continuing support of these riders on the range. *Brokeback Mountain* may have been set in Wyoming, but Colorado cowboys and city boys alike flocked to see it, proving that Jack and Ennis got nothin' on our state when it comes to a love of the West—or each other.

The Crystal Orb

DAVE BROWN

Dave Brown was born and raised in Englewood, Colorado. He attended Catholic grade school and high school. Right after high school, he entered the Christian Brother's monastery. After three years in the order, he realized that he was gay and that the Catholic Church frowned on him. Dave left the order with the firm conviction that Jesus was still his lifelong pal.

Dave met Jim in 1973. Within a week, they became lifetime partners and will remain so for eons.

With the help of his grandfather, Dave taught himself the art of lapidary and had a hobby/business in that field for many years. However, when the writer's bug bit him, he temporarily set gem cutting aside. Only after completing several writing/editing courses and private tutoring from Muriel Olson (editor of several best sellers), and taking extensive courses from Windy Newcastle (PhD–Literature and Creative Writing), did Dave continue writing his provocative gay western series The Legend of the Golden Feather.

Since 1994, Dave has completed and self-published five volumes of his Legend *series, which are being enjoyed across the United States, Canada, Australia, Europe, and Israel. Dave is also publishing the ongoing short story "Emerald Valley" on his Web site, www.goldenfeatherpress.com.*

I FOUND MYSELF STANDING on a faceted crystal plain that curved in all directions. It seemed as big as the Earth.

The orb, extending beyond my sight, had narrow walkways separating the orderly rows of countless windows. Many windows were dark. Some threw out weak light, while others blazed with shafts of dazzling splendor. As I walked down a narrow path, I noticed one pane that lit the upper darkness as far as I could see. I headed toward it.

When I reached that facet, I started to look in, but the brilliant light hurt my eyes. Then I saw a pair of glasses with nearly opaque black

47

lenses placed on a stand beside the window. I grasped the glasses, shoved them on my face, and peered down into the brightness . . .

DAN TREMBLED as he sat in the veranda swing of the white one-storied farmhouse in eastern Colorado. With his clasped hands far down between his legs, he stared out at the wheat fields that flowed up the hill like a dusty green river through sparse forests. He lowered his head and remembered what his lover, Frank, had said to him on the drive there.

"I hope you like Granny. I love her more than anyone. She's cantankerous, opinionated, and religiously righteous, but I'd do anything Granny asked. Granny and her brother are the only family I've ever known."

After stopping the car in front of Granny's house, Frank had turned to him and said, "I'll go in first and set the stage for her to meet you. I hope you don't mind. Why don't you sit on the porch swing?"

Dan stared at a weathered knot in the porch floor. It looked like an old woman screaming. He shuddered. He didn't know if he wanted to meet Granny.

"WHAT'S UP, CHILD?" Granny asked Frank as she rocked in her chair near the idle wood stove. "You act like you shot my prized rooster."

After kissing Granny in greeting, Frank stood before her and swallowed hard. He looked at his feet, his hands shoved into his pants pockets.

"Lordy!" Granny shouted. "If you robbed a bank, I can hide you in the root cellar!"

Frank laughed and then shrugged. "It's nothing like that."

"Get on with it, then!"

Frank looked into Granny's eyes. "I brought my . . . er, friend, Dan, with me. I want you to meet him."

"Friend? What do you mean *friend?*" Granny leaned forward and glared at Frank.

Frank cowered and turned red. "Uh . . . Granny, Dan's my best friend. We've moved in with each other. We're roommates. We . . . we share expenses."

Granny sat back in her rocker, folded her arms, and squinted at her grandson. With puckered lips, she looked Frank up and down, then raised an eyebrow.

Frank shrank under the scrutiny. His knee suddenly pained him, which never happened unless a violent storm approached. He tried to think of all the storms he'd predicted because of the pain in his knee, but none came to mind. He suddenly needed to sit and took an uncertain step toward the closest chair, then stiffly lowered himself into it.

"You're wise to sit right now," Granny said. She clasped her hands, pushed them to her lips, then rested her elbows on the arms of the rocker and peered out the window. "How well do you know this . . . Dan?" She pulled a tissue from the box on the table beside her and gently blew her nose, not once looking at Frank.

Frank squeezed the arm of the chair. "I . . . I know him well. We met in school. We like the same things." He shifted in the straight-back oak chair. "We go to the library together." He shrugged. "Dan comes to the library with me and writes poetry while I read."

"Poetry?" Granny asked. "What manly thing is that?"

"Manly? Er . . . Dan works construction in Colorado Springs. He says writing poetry relaxes him."

"Poetry?" Granny snorted, got up from her rocker, and quickly walked across the parlor. She marched down the short hallway and into her bedroom, slamming the door behind her.

Frank cringed. What was wrong with Granny? She'd never done anything like that before. She'd always confronted everything head on. He tried to see if Dan was still on the porch, but from where he sat, he couldn't see the swing. Was Granny crying? He'd never seen her cry.

Then the bedroom door opened and Granny strode out holding a wrinkled and sagging piece of paper. When she reached Frank, she thrust the paper at him. "Read this," she demanded.

Frank took the limp sheet of paper, immediately recognizing his Great-Uncle Ben's handwriting. He read:

I love you. I love you.
You are more reliable than a John Deere tractor.
You are always there for me.
I want to be there for you always too.
I love you. I love you.
Ben

Frank looked up at Granny. "That's beautiful. But I didn't know Uncle Ben ever had a girlfriend."

Granny snatched the paper out of Frank's hand. "He didn't. He wrote it to Conrad Laden. You know Conrad." She held up the paper. "Is this poetry?"

"Conrad Laden?" Frank whispered. He blinked and looked up at Granny. "Um . . . poetry? I . . . I don't know. You'll have to ask Dan if it's poetry." He pointed at the paper. "Where did you get that? How do you know Uncle Ben wrote it to Conrad?"

"Never mind that! I just know. I found out long before you were born. I got my father's shotgun and ordered Ben out of the house. I told him we would split the acreage. He could have the original 400 acres of the homestead. I also told him that the love he had for Conrad was a sin, and they would both burn in Hell.

"I made sure I was in town the day Ben moved his things out. I didn't want to even be near him anymore. He started living at the old cabin our grandfather built when he first settled here. Conrad moved in with him. I told them, by letter, if they ever came here, I'd cut them in half with the shotgun."

Frank squirmed in his chair. "I wondered why Ben never came here when I was growing up. And why you punished me for visiting him." He wanted to leave. He didn't want Dan to experience Granny's religious wrath. *He* didn't want to experience it. "Granny, I think Dan and I need to get back to Colorado Springs."

"You stay put!" Granny demanded. "You need to know the rest of the story." She waved her hand toward the porch. "Get your Dan in here. He needs to hear this, too."

DAN CHOSE THE CHAIR farthest from Granny's rocker and cringed when she pointed to the chair next to Frank and told him to sit. Then she eyed them both, back and forth, several times before hefting herself out of her rocker. She grabbed the limp paper from the table, walked over to Dan, and handed it to him. "Is this poetry?"

Glad for the diversion, Dan quickly scanned the writing, and then read it again slowly. He looked up at Granny. "It's sort-of poetry. The meaning is very beautiful. Who's Ben?"

Granny snatched the paper out of Dan's hand and walked back to her chair. When she was rocking again, she looked at Dan. "Ben is my brother. He wrote that to his friend Conrad. This was before Frank was born. I tossed Ben out of the house with a shotgun and told him never to come back."

Dan winced and looked around for a shotgun.

"While Frank was growing up," Granny continued, "I forbade him from visiting Ben and Conrad, but he did anyway. I was convinced they were trying to make Frank like they were."

Frank turned to Dan. "They were neat to me. I had no idea they were . . ." He looked at Granny.

"Gay?" Granny asked.

Frank flinched. "Yeah. How do you know that word?"

"Back to the story!" Granny said. "One day Elly Burnhart stopped by . . ."

"How is Miss Elly?"

"Elly died last month."

Frank dropped his head. "I'm sorry. I'll miss her." He looked at Granny. "What did she die of?"

"I think she missed Pete. You know he died last year. They'd been married for over forty years. Elly believed that Pete died from all the diseases he saw on TV commercials." Granny straightened in her rocker. "Anyway, Elly visited one day and told me she had run into Ben and Conrad. She looked hard at me and said that I'd been too rough on Ben and Conrad. She told me that they were the kindest men she had ever known, and that everyone treats them decent because they make our men dream of days gone by, when men could be companions . . . even partners." Granny shrugged and looked at Frank. "Then she said I should go and spend some time with Ben and Conrad, that they would make me laugh and forget that your Grandpa Fred died so long ago."

Granny stared at Dan, then back at Frank. "Are you two ready for the rest of the story?"

"I am," Dan said instantly.

Granny looked at him and cocked an eyebrow. Her face softened just a bit and the room seemed to brighten. "Well, I went to visit Ben and Conrad. When I got there, they were nowhere to be found. I rang the dinner triangle on the porch, and in a few minutes, here they came, riding fast. Ben got there first and stopped his horse in front of the house and stayed in the saddle. He glared at me and said, 'What do *you* want?'"

"Did you bring your shotgun?" Frank interrupted.

Granny snatched a tissue and lightly blew her nose. From where Dan sat, he noticed the side of her mouth turn up in a smile. The room seemed to brighten even more.

After Granny folded the tissue and wiped her mouth, she said, "No. I didn't bring it, but I thought about it."

"What happened?" Frank asked, leaning forward in his chair.

Granny frowned at him. "Don't be hasty!" She dropped the tissue in the nearby crock and looked from Frank to Dan. Then she examined the flower embroidery around the hem of her dress and smoothed the dress over her knees. "When Conrad walked his horse beside Ben, he asked me the same question—about the shotgun. I told them I hadn't come to shoot them, just to see what they were about.

"Ben laughed at me and said, 'Likely story.' He accused me of being a holier-than-thou bigot. He said that my God is one of hate and judgment and that he wanted no part of that kind of god, or of me. He told me to leave and never come back."

"Gods come and Gods go, but love is an eternal flow," Dan said. He looked at the floor when Granny glared at him.

"You are *going* to hear the rest of the story," Granny told Dan. "You can write a poem about it later."

Frank looked at Dan and saw him flip a number-one thumb at Granny, wink, and grin. Then he looked at Granny and saw a faint nod. What was going on here? Why did everything seem to be brighter in here?

Granny continued her story.

"I stood my ground and told Ben I wasn't leaving because I'd promised Elly I'd visit them. They hadn't come to her funeral, after all. Conrad said that his sister's funeral was the same day in Denver, but Ben said he wouldn't have gone to Elly's funeral anyway, knowing I'd be there.

"It was Conrad who dismounted first. He tied his horse, walked by me, and opened the cabin door. He asked me in to see how they had fixed up the old homestead. Ben just sat in his saddle and scowled." Granny shook her head. "Ben always was a scowler."

After rocking a few times, Granny turned her head and stared out the window again. "I was amazed at how homey the old cabin looked. It was even more enchanting than I'd remembered it as a child. All the original furniture was still there, and what was new fit right in." Then she looked back at Frank and Dan, swept her hand at the parlor, and added, "It looked nothing like this dump, but I've been into wheat, not furniture." She pushed herself to her feet. "Come into the kitchen. We'll have a little refreshment while I continue the story."

While Frank and Dan picked out chairs next to each other at the far side of the round wooden table, Granny went to a cupboard. When she approached the table, she held a bottle of Jack Daniels and three small glasses that had originally contained pimento cheese spread. Dan glanced at Frank with wide eyes.

"Don't look at him like that," Granny said. "We'll all need a nip for what's coming." She seated herself across from the pair, poured a two-finger shot into each glass, and slid two glasses across the table. The men followed Granny's lead and sipped the whiskey.

Frank coughed and his eyes teared.

"I can mix it with water," Granny offered.

"That's okay," Frank gasped. "It's fine. I'm not used to hard liquor."

Granny took another sip. "Now then, where was I?"

"You were describing Ben and Conrad's cabin," Dan offered.

"That's right." Granny smiled and took another sip. "I looked around the two rooms for filthy magazines, but didn't see any. The bedroom was spotless, and I was surprised to see the old crucifix Grandpa had carved still hanging above the bed.

"Just as I was about to comment on the crucifix being there, Ben walked into the room. 'You won't find any porn in this house,' he said. 'And we don't roll around in bed all the time, either, like you and your church friends think. We work hard, we love Jesus, and we love each other.'" She took a sip of her drink. "I'll never forget those words."

Granny closed her eyes for a moment, then continued. "The only thing I could think of to do was point at the coverless New Testament on a bedside table. I asked them how they could say they loved Jesus when the New Testament was ripped up like it was. Ben told me it wasn't ripped up, but they had torn away all the other books since they were someone else's words and not Jesus'.

"I was stunned. My church had always considered Paul's words as God's words, but I suddenly realized that Ben was right." Granny shrugged. "Of course, I didn't tell him that. I just started off on a tirade of Old Testament verses to condemn the two of them. Ben stopped me again and said, 'Jesus fulfilled the Old Testament. Stop quoting all those old Jewish customs. We aren't Jewish.'

"It was then that Conrad came into the bedroom. I hadn't even noticed that he'd left. He asked me to stay for dinner—ham hocks and beans."

"Granny, that's your favorite!" Frank said.

Granny smiled at Frank. "You're right, and it did entrap me. Besides, I thought if I stayed a little longer, I might get through to Ben how horrible his lifestyle was."

After another sip of Jack Daniels, Granny went on. "Dinner was delicious, if I say so myself. Conrad is a wonderful cook. When all my Bible verses failed to convert them to my way of thinking, I decided to take Ben's advice and quit trying. That's when Ben brought up a few memories of our childhood. Pretty soon, I was joining in with memories of my own. I even admitted to Ben that it was not Johnny Sanders who pushed him into the roses from behind while playing Blind Man's Bluff. It was me that did it." Granny laughed. "Ben pretended to be mad, but then he burst out laughing. He had given Johnny a black eye for that."

Both Frank and Dan looked around. A bright glow seemed to flood the kitchen.

Granny chugged the remaining whiskey and plunked down her glass. "I stayed at their house until eleven o'clock that night and had to drive home in the dark. I spent the rest of the night thinking about Ben and Conrad and how they never once talked nasty to each other the way Fred and I did while we were married. I also realized that I had never been waited on hand and foot by any man in my life, and both of them treated me like a queen."

Dan snickered. "Queens waiting on a queen," he said and downed his whiskey.

"Ben and Conrad are *not* queens," Granny snapped. "They are both men, even though Ben still writes poetry." She raised her eyebrow at Dan. "Like you."

Frank took another sip of his whiskey, choked, and shoved the glass aside. "When did all this happen, anyway?"

Smiling at Frank, Granny said, "The day after Elly's funeral. It turned out that Elly was right. Those two are well respected all over the area. They even volunteer three days a week at the Sunshine Senior Home. They said they'd most likely be living there in a few years, and they might as well help out until then."

Granny scooted back her chair and stood. "We should be going now."

"Going where?" Frank asked.

"To Ben and Conrad's. If you two are planning to live together, you have to learn from them how to do it properly." Granny winked at Dan. "Maybe you can teach Ben how to write poetry."

Then, laughing in the brilliant light that surrounded them, the three went outside and piled into Frank's car . . .

I TURNED AWAY from the crystal facet, took off the black glasses, placed them on the stand, and rubbed my eyes. For a long time, I stood beside the window and looked up at how far its glory penetrated the darkness.

●   ●   ●

Urban Cowboy

Carolee Laughton

Carolee Laughton is a freelance and fiction writer living in Denver, Colorado. She enjoys writing current and historical western fiction with diverse, multilayered characters and themes. Carolee has recently completed her first novel about a woman outlaw.

*S*HE CALLED ME "COWBOY" as she walked by and smiled at me. But I was never a "real" cowboy. A bull named Meditation fell on me at the Colorado Gay Rodeo in Golden, ending my fantasy as a cowboy rodeo rider forever. Never imagined that a mere five seconds could affect the rest of my life. The bull spun sharply around in the air and landed off balance in the arena. Couldn't stay on him. My last memory of that ride was eating dirt, a blur of him falling on top of me, and blackness.

I've been stuck in this wheelchair for six long years, berating myself. Shit. Why did I feel I had something else to prove to the world? Wasn't transitioning from female to male challenge enough? Since I was five years old, my only other dream was riding rodeo bulls. Testosterone freed me to live this life. I had to try.

The accident cut me down when I was only 25. Can't totally give up my cowboy dream, though, because I still dress the part, but now it's always in black.

So that's the way she saw me when she came walking down Arapahoe that day on her way home from work. She had to pass by us all as we were catching breezes and a few rays, talking among ourselves or waiting for the damned bus for the handicapped to take us someplace.

At first I thought, *Here's an able-bodied bitch feeling sorry for us crips.* But I was wrong. She genuinely liked people; you could see it in

those gray eyes of hers. She moved through our group like a good cutting horse.

She waved to Jimmy the Drooler, my nickname for him, and asked an enfeebled woman I knew only as Martha how she was. Then she came by little ol' life-damaged me. It made me smile just to look at her. Couldn't talk to her either—fuck it, the bull ended that, too.

She was in her mid, maybe late 20s, with medium-brown hair cascading in one smooth river down her back, rippling with her when she walked. As she moved toward me, she rolled her hips in unconscious grace, not like some women I see who stomp down the street, their bodies quivering like bouncing, bulky packages.

The first thing I did is what I do with all new people: try to guess what she did for a living and learn her name. After all, I had plenty of time to kill.

Figured out that she always drove her car into work on Mondays and Wednesdays. The parking lot was just beyond the building where I lived. Sometimes my therapy schedule didn't jibe with her work schedule. Other times it rained or snowed, so I couldn't be there. Sometimes I waited outside in vain, and she didn't come at all.

I wondered, just a little, maybe, if she missed me, too, when she came by and didn't see me. Sure, I wanted to love her! Who wouldn't love someone so beautiful and kind? There was another reason why she was important to me, too. But I just couldn't name it.

At first I thought she might work for one of the phone companies, or perhaps a teller at one of the banks on 17th Street. I lucked out one night when I overheard her talking to a friend about office problems and learned she was a receptionist in one of the small offices in lower downtown Denver.

Don't it just beat all—as she walked by, she gave her little wave and called out in a soft, friendly voice, "Hey, Cowboy, how are you doing tonight?"

My head rolls to the side, which frustrates me no end, and I can't lift it up much. I strained to but just couldn't do it, and she and her friend continued on. I wanted to look her straight in the eye! Wanted to pound my fist on the armrest of the chair. Couldn't do that either.

It seemed like a real waste of the state's money, but I went to physical therapy every week. Gave me something to look forward to. Most times the therapist just went through the whole physical routine. Nothing ever changed. Until now.

"You know, your neck has more responsiveness today. Just what have you been up to, anyway?"

Could Gray Eyes be my Lady Luck? The exercises the therapist gave me I now did with a vengeance. I did more repetitions and struggled holding my head up straight until my neck muscles throbbed in weariness.

Took quite a ribbing from the other guys in therapy saying I was stuck up, looking at myself in the mirror all the time. They didn't know that when I looked in the mirror, it was her I really saw.

I just wanted those gray eyes to look and really see *me*. I wanted my lady to know that there really was a person inside the broken shell she saw. God Almighty above, I wanted so much to be able to spring up from this chair, throw my arms around her, and dance the two-step all the way to Coors Field! That's what I wanted. What I had to be satisfied with was a whole 'nother story.

Got antsy when I didn't see her for a couple of weeks and wondered if she'd left her job. All this effort might've been for nothing.

But the following Monday, there she was, walking up Arapahoe right on schedule—hoo boy, was I ever relieved.

Just as she came up in front of me, I put on my best "howdy partner" smile and pulled my neck up tall as I could. Her words were like the sweetgrass smell in a newly mowed field.

"Hey, Cowboy, you're doing great," she said, her voice full of surprise. As she leaned down, lightly touching my shoulder, her eyes met mine. And I realized that she didn't see a crip—she saw me. The wheelchair didn't matter to her; should it matter to me?

Even as stupid fantasies passed through my mind, I realized then that what she represented was a new challenge to me to overcome— just like my evolution to manhood. Just like that bull. I took that challenge, overcame it, and won. As I smiled at her, I was also smiling at myself to think that the spirit I thought had died that day in the arena had been in me all along.

• • •

It's not surprising that Colorado attracts creative types of all stripes. Writers, artists, musicians, and performers migrate to the state not only to enjoy the mix of urban arts culture and (almost) pristine wilderness, but also to be inspired in their work. Katharine Lee Bates was so inspired that she wrote the first version of "America the Beautiful," one of the nation's most beloved tributes to America, after taking in the view from Pikes Peak and later expanded it into the version that we now sing.

And yes, we do claim her as our own—Bates, a professor at Wellesley College, had a 25-year relationship with fellow Wellesley faculty member Katharine Coman. The two lived together until Coman's death in 1915. Although the exact nature of the relationship remains unknown, the poetry that Bates wrote to and about Coman leaves little question about the love that Bates felt for her longtime companion.

How ironic it is that in a state that has sent Marilyn Musgrave and Wayne Allard, the two primary sponsors of the anti-gay Federal Marriage Amendment, to Congress; in a state that passed the discriminatory Amendments 2 and 43 and struck down a domestic partnership initiative; and in a state that is home to some of the most powerful anti-gay activists in the country, a woman-loving woman stood atop Pikes Peak and wrote a song that the entire nation cherishes, and that many have argued should replace "The Star Spangled Banner" as the U.S. national anthem. Colorado is just full of surprises.

But Bates is not the only one who has been moved to creativity by the landscape of our state. There is enough in Colorado to keep our poets busy for a very long time.

Native

SUNSHINE DEMPSEY

Sunshine Dempsey grew up in Boulder and graduated from Colorado State University with a Bachelor of Arts in English and Art History. She currently resides in Longmont.

You and I are blessed creatures, Sara—
finding our affection for one another easily
written in the woodsmoke hieroglyphics
of our separate
October canyons.

We were raised liberally
on redrock sandstone and bricks—
we watched snow settle pink on
childhood Flatirons,
blue flakes falling after sundown,
wet streets in Glenwood and Durango and Manitou

You were young here,
grabbing wild-maned horses,
riding the prairie crashing
into the foothills like a
goddamn legend

Your blood is thick with tallgrass
and yucca,
you are the boy above treeline,
struck by lightning,
the long train whistle—you are
sulfur
in these mountains—
you are these mountains:
broad-shouldered,
obstinate

You bring the stars and moon
to pasture:
I am not sure
they can find their way alone.

How can I tell you
I see that connection?

•   •   •

Landfire

Gretchen Haley

Gretchen Haley is a queer bisexual social justice artist who resides in Denver with her partner, Carri, and their one-year-old daughter, Gracie Ella. Gretchen received her Master of Arts in Theatre from the University of Colorado, Boulder, and her Bachelor of Arts in Theatre Arts from the University of Puget Sound, where her work and studies focused on dramaturgy, solo performance, and rehearsal. Her writing has been published in the journal Matter, *the performance journal* On-Stage Studies, *and the queer newspaper* Weird Sisters, *as well as in her self-produced chapbook,* Mourning Agenda.

She is passionate about gardening, Anusara yoga, adoptive families, poetry, and community-based collaborative social-justice-fueled arts, and she is currently applying to seminary to become a Unitarian Universalist minister.

Gretchen moved to Colorado in 1997 from the rain-soaked Pacific Northwest (Port Angeles, Washington—via Tacoma), without ever having previously visited, to attend her master's program. Although she completed her degree in 2000, she has no intention of ever leaving this landlocked state or its annual 300 days of beautiful and dry sunshine.

Peering across thick
ancient cliffs, one
thousand miles of land
the dry white salt of
the Utah ocean
the red delicate
hopeful arches and
tacky Nevada
lights against the
brown desert sky
this is what I mean by geography:

The memory of up and down my body a phantom touch
the haunting of a few stolen days
you now unwillingly going west
30,000 feet your tray table up
I lay down to sleep I taste
you on my lips feel
you on my legs
between my fingers
like the plains
I did not know
how much more beautiful
the mountains could make me

Waiting for hot dogs
and black bean burgers
green chile and soft
burritos, sitting in the grass
watching Washington
Park drivers squeezing
along the narrow
roads, you move back into
me with your feet
dangling in the
baby pool
as if topography means more than this:
Standing on the bridge
looking out over
Boulder Creek, leaning
into the rail, leaning
into you, the
water forceful
impatient drawing
down below us,
I take your hand
I lead you along a

secret path and we
kiss in the trees
looking over your
shoulder in intimate
espionage, protecting
innocent civilians
from catching a glimpse
of two girls in love

You have your ticket
in your hand, you have
your name on my lips
along the Front Range
you look for
residency and
crystal balls,
write dissertations
on cement walls and
iron gates,
San Francisco fog
and east bay winds,
I walk towards Devil's Thumb
lining up states
emotional and otherwise
alphabetically, parenthetically,
the valleys, the dry
cracked earth shedding
skin, layer upon
layer of tears, fears—
you know the sound of
your hands,
move their way along
the pavement
the placement the
scorched severed land

that was my heart
environmentalist
still beating it moves
and twists, wondering:
> *does this land matter*
> *enough, does this march*
> *endure wars and highways,*
> *seasons and slippings*
> *stretchmarks and birthmarks*
> *simmering*
> *along the reservoir*
> *I hear the secret*
> *fire spreading—*
> *falling, falling*

If you can believe it
when I was younger
living in the rainforest
I was sure
tumbleweeds were a
myth used in cartoons
and old westerns—
my northwest streets lined
with wet trees—now
sometimes they get caught
on my pant leg or
under my tire, huge
tangles of dried
unwanted mess, you
have me
here along this
continental divide
this shifting plate, we
balance along, one
foot in front of the other,
onward

● ● ●

Mountainside

ANGELA PALERMO

*A transplant to Colorado, **Angela Palermo** is a writer, performer, and activist living in Denver. She has published poems in the* LAWCHA Newsletter, Main Street Free Press, Slam This! *(CU Boulder's slam poetry anthology), and* Transgender Tapestry. *She has performed at Lady Fest Out West in Denver and was the featured performer at Boston's Gender Crash in October 2005.*

An out transsexual woman, Angela wrote her own monologue for a performance of The Vagina Monologues *in February 2006. She is presently collaborating with her partner, Sandra Azcarate, on* Mujeres del Sol, *a self-published comic book set in a dystopic near-future. The first issue is available at www.mujeresdelsol.com. She is committed to ending all forms of sexual and domestic violence, volunteering with the Rape Assistance and Awareness Program (RAAP) and Colorado Anti-Violence Program (CAVP). Unlike some progressive activists, Angela is eagerly awaiting the fall of Western "civilization."*

Ascending through a forest
slowly scanning the surroundings
eyes eager for beauty
wonder
green life opening to the sky
making love
adoring the other
arms outstretched in worship
silent prayers of creation
gentle cool breeze rustling
shifting the boughs
whispers through the pines
susurrant

murmuring incantation
song of survival
endurance
a chorus of sounds sights smells
sensations delightful
and I
requiescence in motion
winding
traversing
doubling back
taking it all in
hoping for nothing more
enjoying the journey

• • •

Spring at Gem Lake

(for Annie)

MELANIE STAFFORD

Melanie Stafford is Managing Editor of Paradigm Publishers in Boulder, Colorado. She is also a feminist activist, having served as president of the Women's Lobby of Colorado, state coordinator of the National Organization for Women Colorado chapter, and the South Central Regional Director on the National NOW Board. She has been writing poetry since she could hold a pen.

Two girls wade
into the mica clear lake
rolled up jeans wet anyway
long hair catching the corners of laughing mouths
hands brushing like pine boughs in the breeze

They don't yet know how their beloved voices
will reverberate along the crags of memory;
how they will someday long for just such a shore
from which to skip stones
side by side.

Two women wade
into the melted crystal current
numb toes seeking sun-warmed shoals
hair glinting like fool's gold in a newly thawed spring
hands longing to tangle the way their hair once did

They cast stories in perfect arcs
of just such lake-washed days,
their words circling back further and further
until the ripples caress
those barefoot girls.

• • •

Planting Your Poppies

DEENA LARSEN

Deena Larsen is an electronic writer with over thirty intricate works only available on a computer. She works as a technical writer for the federal government. Her poems are part of a series of poems written to her wife while recovering from a severe illness. More of Deena's writing can be found at www.deenalarsen.net.

*I keep moving the pots to arrange
the growing effect. Your bright-orange
poppies don't quite fit with my cool
magenta and white cosmos.*

*So I'm putting your poppies a bit behind
the yellow and golden brown iris
for the full effect of the sun.*

*I dig in the loam, redolent from centuries
of leaves piled from the neighbor's sycamore tree
(a rarity here, feeding from the secret spring that runs
through the dry city from the Platte—a tiny grinning
line of green-cracked basements and tall trees).*

*I break the dirt from years previous.
Sift out the rocks and place them carefully to one side.
I tire easily and rest slowly in the ground.*

You come out in time
to plant our wood violets—
the ones that have heard
our past confessions.

We leave them as silent
witnesses to our passion,
bordering the pungent sweet william.

•   •   •

Not everyone who comes to Colorado is immediately—or ever—enraptured. For example, East Coast sensibilities don't always mix with western hospitalities. What some see as room to breathe can appear to others as empty space—dry, barren, and lonely. For all of us, GLBT or not, our sense of place is fashioned by our experiences, our preferences, and what gives us comfort and strength, and the attachments that hold us in place might not be the ones that we expected. But yet we remain.

Reprise

Laura Givens

Laura Givens moved to Denver in 2006 to work as a union organizer. Shortly thereafter, she left the labor movement in order to win back her weekends and is now studying massage therapy. This is her first published piece.

I HAVE A RECURRING DREAM about Kate. She has split where we grew up. She is dressed like an anchorwoman and speaks in deep, clipped tones. She smokes and paces and makes me think of traffic and cancer and alcoholism. Western Kate is Colorado, where I went to prove that Kate wouldn't follow. That Kate doesn't exist, of course, but Pennsylvania talks like she does—talks to me about a Colorado Kate made of open skies and horseback rides who can't wait to see me again after all these years.

Pennsylvania is trying desperately to give me a makeover before Colorado gets here. She needs to pretty me up to impress her Western self because she's in love with me and wants me to be happy with Colorado and wants Colorado to be smitten with me. She tells me you have to set the scene. You have to stage things properly. I only half-realize that it's ludicrous for her to try so hard to set me up with herself. I am too confused to know where to begin to talk her out of this nonsense.

She goes on and on about how wonderful Colorado Kate is and how well we'll get along. I say, of course, we are getting along, aren't we? Has she really missed me? But Pennsylvania is too shy to answer. She is talking around and over and under my admiration, which she pretends is entirely for the West. The East is the past, our home, and she treats it as dry and dead.

She keeps introducing me to beautiful women who are embracing each other and flirting with me. I know she's testing me, so I don't react to them, I try not to look at them as I listen to her lecture me on how I have to be myself—she won't put up with nonsense once she comes back from Colorado. I begin to think she knows she's making it all up—that she's tricking me because she is angry that she is not made of sunshine, and mountains that are new enough to be majestic, and snow that melts before the traffic turns it black. She's invented this Western self so that she won't have to see me, or so that she can pretend I can't see her. This impossible logic makes sense in my sleep, and I realize that we have to have these tricks because it's too late to honestly have each other.

PENNSYLVANIA KEEPS TRYING to make me wear a dress, insisting that Colorado expects me to put my best foot forward. I start telling her the story about the time I had to fight to get out of wearing a ball gown.

"I told them dresses were drag for me and you can't make me do drag. They thought I was joking, so they just told me 'It's a *ball*, Hannah, you have to wear a ball *gown*. Come on, it'll be fun.' But I kept telling them I wouldn't do it, they could fire me if they liked, but I wouldn't do it, Kate . . ."

I keep talking and talking and am far too emotional and expressive, and I start doing horrible unflattering impressions of my co-workers, and eventually notice that I'm rambling. I stop and am relieved that Kate is on her cell phone, deaf to my speech. She's piling gown after gown into my arms and making me parade around. She's giving me wigs and scarves and stolen cosmetics. I want to cry and tell her to stop this, but I love her, so if this is what she really wants, I'll let her do it.

Finally, once I look like somebody out of *Hairspray*, Kate deems the makeover a success. I begin to wonder if she has some weird beehive fetish . . . and then we're on a cruise ship and Pennsylvania is saying Colorado missed her flight and won't be here, and I keep thinking "but you *are,* you're right here . . ."

SO I HAVE THIS DREAM a lot, with some minor variations in hair and makeup. The main thing is that she always tries to put me in wigs and dresses and heels, and I always let her, knowing that it's her insecurity, not mine, and wishing she wanted to dress me up in tweed suits or argyle sweater vests or smoking jackets. In my sleep I reinvent her reinventing me, and we never do anything except wait for our original selves to come back to us so that we can live happily ever after.

I have a lot of glamour nightmares, but the ones starring Kate are the worst. I want it to mean something, because I dream it so often. I want it to answer something, or fix something—or I want it just once to end with Colorado Kate coming and laughing and asking me why I'm wearing such a silly outfit, and then we fade into music and clouds and sunsets. It could be a proper dream, and I would wake up thinking that first love is magic.

But instead I wake up depressed, thinking that first love has a disproportionate hold on my unconscious. I wake up wanting first love back, because it's the least attainable thing in the world. But instead I have this stupid room in the middle of the night, in the middle of my life, in the middle of fucking Colorado. And Kate has her Pennsylvania self, two hours ahead of me and probably awake already, stuck in traffic maybe, chain smoking and drinking coffee and applying mascara in her car.

And then I'm brought out of this melancholy crap by Molly's sweet sleep-breathing. Molly, who was born here and takes all the space and sunshine and scenery for granted. Who thinks Pittsburgh is the most depressing place in the world and hardly sees how the Poconos dare call themselves mountains. In the morning, when I tell her I had the glamour dream again, she will laugh at me and ask what I was forced to wear this time. She'll laugh harder when I tell her about the beehive and fake eyelashes and fashion mole. Then she'll smile and say she envies me these vivid dreams because she can never remember hers.

• • •

Give Me a Home

Peter D. Clarke

Peter D. Clarke grew up in New England and New York and so he believes in difficulty. He thinks the written word is sublime. His literary influences are an unholy goulash of Sylvia Plath, Oscar Wilde, William Peter Blatty, Yoko Ono, L. Frank Baum, and Pauline Réage—and that's just for starters. By profession he is a social worker and not the international film star he always imagined, but c'est la guerre.

MY DREAMS AND LONGING are in shades of green. Out the windows of my mind are the soft, rounded mountains I remember, thick with trees—the hemlock, the countless oaks and maples mottled with lichen. I imagine biting into leaves, finding them crisp and bitter. There is a smell of growth in the air, and it is sweet. The forest floor is mossy and mystical with life. My skin is moistened by the very air.

The reality of Colorado, from where I dream now, is nearly the opposite. The hills are angular, the color of mustard and white gold, and they are bare. Those trees that do sprout from the ground and persevere are noxious. A good number of them are the offspring of transplants, first brought here to serve as windbreaks. Branches sprout from every part of their trunks like wild hairs, without design, and they crisscross pointlessly. They are ugly by any aesthetic. The flat grasslands lie so open and naked that they cannot hide the litter tossed from cars. They look poor and shabby. Plastic grocery sacks flutter on barbed wire fences. The air is parched. My skin is withering. My hands look like those of an old rancher, lined and weathered, and I am not old.

It was drought and experience that led me to realize what I had given up and left behind, and that was many years after moving West. Before then, I was content with the dry heat and the soaring skies. They were exotic to me. The differences in the flora and weather and the landscape performed a sleight-of-hand trick that kept me interested for a long time.

From the East Coast, I had pictured Colorado as green and lush, like Vermont. In the movies, the state was just a snowy mountain playground. No camera ever trained its eye on the deserts and prairies that comprise most of it. Until seeing Denver in person, I had to make it up. Someone had once told me that Denver was "in a bowl," and so in my mind it was nestled in the heart of the Rockies and surrounded by evergreen forests, like Innsbruck or Shangri-La. That bowl, as it turned out, is merely a depression in the plains that allows brown car exhaust to engulf it on even the sunniest winter days, the way fog clings to London.

HE WAS WHITE ON TOP, like Mount Evans, and tall, with blue eyes—a silver dandy with an eye for young and vulnerable things. I was working in the Doubleday bookstore in Grand Central Station. Twenty-five, nearly two decades his junior, and not the least bit ambitious or focused, I was Peter Pan, with no idea how to grow up. He approached me with his big smile, valanced by a silver mustache, and asked me about a new book by a psychotherapist. I just happened to know it—it must have been kismet—and I was happy to discuss the topic further over dinner.

Timothy was in the doctoral program in Social Work at Yeshiva University. He was not a Jew. He was an ordained Lutheran minister who had come to New York from Omaha in order to pursue bigger and better things, including the enormous pool of men the City had to offer.

I understood why someone like Timothy would want to come to New York. Where else would a person with any sense want to be? I had moved there from Connecticut at the age of seventeen, so in love with the City that I ached all over. It never occurred to me that I could ever leave it. It was the center of the universe, and I had the lease on a rent-stabilized apartment on a tree-lined block in Chelsea, when such a thing was in the realm of possibility for a ne'er-do-well.

Timothy had a bourgeoning psychotherapy practice. He helped the lost and suffering reform their lives. His past as a Podunk prairie minister, married with children, had made him earnest and wise. The hurts he had endured when his wife divorced him, spiriting his children away, humbled him and made him sympathetic. He knew about life the hard way.

There is a fable about the sun and the wind, and which force of nature can more quickly make a man on the road remove his cloak. Timothy was like that sun. His warmth and wisdom undressed me, and I basked in his light, and I followed him as if he were a compass. I let him lead me. I let him love me, even though I was unsure of what it was like to love in return the way an adult can love. I felt like a petulant teen to his guiding fatherly good intentions, an ungrateful brat who was smart enough to recognize a good thing, but not smart enough to love it.

I trusted him to tell me what was wrong with me, and he frequently did. When I returned the favor, he told me, "That was a cruel thing to say." He saw to my character building and I told myself that nothing easy was worth fighting for.

In a matter of months I moved in with him. I stopped going out so often at night. I was gradually and willingly domesticated.

BEFORE LONG WE WERE TALKING about moving out of New York. I still can't believe the St. Vitus Dance that overtook me, but I found myself discontented with my City. Timothy found his settling apartment too old and confining. He wanted to live in a place with "square corners." Prices were skyrocketing. The New York that President Ford had famously told to "Drop Dead" was back in fashion. There wasn't a sidewalk free of construction shelters as more and more high-rises clattered upwards. The subways were crammed with newcomers. It seemed that the personal New York I had known was under invasion by ambitious Wall Street brokers and other opportunists. I was the jilted lover; Manhattan was forsaking me for more enterprising types. For a time we looked at buying a house in the suburbs, driving as far as Tarrytown with the intent of commuting. But the prices of houses were out of reach and my meager income offered no help to Timothy.

THAT NEXT SUMMER he proposed a car trip across the country—at his expense, of course. For a month we drove across the big flat heartland, where the horizon's periphery was not obscured by trees, then up to the wilds of the Northern Rockies, across to California. I saw natural wonders I had never dreamed of. The sky was a shade of blue I'd only seen in storybooks. Pools of hot water hissed and boiled, but looked so crystalline that I was tempted to submerge myself. Switchbacks brought to mind the thrills of man-made roller coasters. We drove right through giant sequoias straddling the road. Twisted pines clung to bluffs over the Pacific, forming picture-postcard views. Palm trees grew outside.

I remember one afternoon as we crossed Nevada in deep August. The scenery outside the car was bleak, like the surface of the moon, but hoary with dead brush. It was immense and dangerous. One could die in it. The hot air whipped at me, and I was flooded with sadness and unable to hold it in. I turned my head to the right, as though I were looking out the window or sleeping. But I couldn't quiet the sounds of my weeping.

I thought that I was getting away with it for a while, until Timothy asked, "What is it?"

A few minutes passed before I was able to speak.

"Why are you taking me on this trip?" I sniveled, overwhelmed that he would spend so much money and be willing to share this adventure with me.

"Because I love you," he answered.

I suppose I took his hand and was grateful, and I kept on crying.

I LEARNED THAT THERE WAS LIFE beyond New Jersey, a fact I'd found impossible to believe until seeing it for myself. In Colorado Springs, we stopped at a supermarket to get food and drink for the day's drive. The market was brand new and expansive, making the Red Apple and D'Agostino stores of Manhattan puny and filthy by comparison. The produce department was fruited like a bacchanalian feast, and the prices were astonishingly low. It was like finding some unknown treasure trove. Why hadn't I ever heard of this before? It made us giddy, and we started to make disparaging comments about New York as we headed back to the close quarters and responsibilities we'd left behind for a month.

We decided to have a look at Denver. Denver was the largest city with proximity to the great wilds, and it seemed the natural choice as a place to live. Ideally, one could enjoy the benefits of both the frontier and urban living. In the fall I started graduate school at Yeshiva to study social work like a dutiful protégé. In October we flew out to Denver to see what there was to see.

By the following summer, I was a Denverite.

The low price of fruit and the afternoon thunderstorms every day kept me astonished. Summer nights were cool, and the autumn was hot. The turning leaves were just one color—very bright yellow—and they fluttered against the blue sky like bangles on a gypsy. Heavy snows at Christmas harkened back to those I'd known as a child. With these things, I could ignore the bad local theater and the lack of repertory movie houses, the awful clubs and scarcity of counterculture.

Traffic was negligible as I knew it, but a car was an absolute necessity. I lost the pleasure of walking everywhere. Downtown felt like a wasteland after the clamor of Manhattan. The office towers cast shadows over empty streets as though there had been a mass evacuation. It was eerie, and I turned a blind eye to what I didn't like because of the shocking newness of it all.

Lots of locals, like the men wearing suits with bolos and cowboy boots, referred to Denver as a "cow town." And it did strike me as twenty years behind the times, but wasn't that sort of charming? I considered myself a benefit to the voting bloc, determined to turn around the repressive political climate. When the city was criticized, I came to its defense, saying, "Even the *cheap* apartments here come with dishwashers and swimming pools."

I bravely bore the dead plains of April and the sight of tumbleweeds rolling across the street, even when my senses longed for just a whisper of green and the sight of a dogwood tree blackened by warm rain. The dead, brown prairie persisted on and on. Proof of winter's tenacious clutch hit me in the form of a terrible flu come May.

We assumed the mortgage on a little house in the curvy streets of Krisana Park and put down roots. I learned to garden and I did what I could to re-create a bower on the high, wide reach.

Like a real grown-up couple, we settled into careers during the week, and on Sundays we had relations. On one side of me were the mountains. On the other side was Timothy. The two provided me with a compass, and I always knew what was true and where I was.

THE SIGHT OF BIG MOUNTAINS inspires wonder. They put you in your place if you let them. Every time I saw them I felt a little thrill. Not long after moving to Denver, I asked a woman I knew, "Does the view still get to you?"

"Not so much," she said.

"I can't imagine that," I said.

"Well, I've lived here for twelve years."

I declared, "I know I'll always feel this way about them." I believed it.

I don't remember what year it was that I stopped feeling a sense of wonder. It was at least after the seven years I spent with Timothy, after he'd grown discontented and no longer realized any payoff in me, and I found myself saying I couldn't stand in the way of his happiness and would leave him. Ashamed that I had bungled such a gift as him, I signed away my portion of the house. Torn out by the roots, I moved to a tiny apartment downtown, one that had no pool or dishwasher. And then I looked around. All the things I'd told myself to make Denver appealing, whether true or enhancements of the truth, were torn from my eyes like a veil—or rather like many veils, in layers, as one secret after another came to light and Peter Pan lost innocence after innocence. While I felt I'd failed Timothy, people came forth with details that I hadn't known. Godly Timothy, it turned out, was a very flawed and mortal man.

The world came crashing down with each disclosure. The deceptions, the chicanery, the strategizing, the fraud: it turned out that I was less a failure than I was a fool. The compass I'd lived by was in smithereens. The shards in my heart said, "Find your own way again."

IN DENVER, people still say "back East," acknowledging the pioneers' roots, as though we have all left something of ourselves at Plymouth Rock. I visited back East—home—as much as possible, to find refuge in the aftermath of Timothy. Home was a balm, and I came to see it with

84

new eyes, the way some people view their ancestral nations. It was there that my roots remained unbroken.

Like the survivor of a cyclone, I chose to rebuild where I was. It only occurred to me in passing to move back. That seemed next to impossible. My little apartment in Chelsea was gone. New York had forgotten me and moved on. And my life in Denver had too much momentum to pretend otherwise. I found there was enough in the debris to salvage.

The particulars of my life—love, family, home, occupation, friends—have re-rooted and flourished. I have a house of my own that I share with someone I love. And I have a son who was born in Colorado and is attached to his homeland. Denver even has more *haute* to its altitude, much more like a real city now. It is the fact that all these things are experienced against a great barren expanse that troubles me as I go on. As much as they fulfill me, the realities of my life tether me also.

I take solace in my gardening, in working the earth, still trying to re-create the verdancy of home here, with mixed results. I dig up ferns in the woods behind my parents' house and plant them in my own yard with a great deal of hope. "*Qui transtulit sustinet,*" my father reminds me. It is the old state motto for Connecticut: "*Who transplants sustains.*" The thin air is so dry, the temperatures so extreme, and the sun so bright—what calls for sun in most places seeks shade at altitude. And now the climate I once admired has evaporated into drought. Afternoon thunderstorms in the summer are an occasion. Christmas is as warm as May Day. The foothills never truly turn green anymore, and they are frequently on fire. The great aquifer beneath the Front Range is being tapped to keep the lawns alive.

On one visit home, my mother mentioned that she finds herself longing for the waters of her youth. She had my father drive us by the blue-green waters of Lake Quassapaug, where she swam as a girl, and she talked about having a little house on its bank. "I think as we get older, we yearn for water," she said.

The souls who took to wagons and rolled into the vastness have my tears. There was no turning back for them. Most never saw their roots again. They hadn't the means to return for a drink of the waters they left behind. I sometimes feel as I think they might have. I liken myself to a mail-order bride who rode the rails west, in hope of a better life, only to become trapped by the circumstances of what was found here. I have more options than they did, it's true, but it seems that I have left home for good.

The view outside my windows is not the view I want. The frustration is endurable and mostly quiet. I recently reconnected with an old New York friend. He never left the City and was curious about the West. I mentioned the Arapaho Indians who once roamed here, never staying in one place for long. I mused about returning East as an old man, so that I could be buried in my native soil, where the cemeteries are very old and staid and green. I don't want to be buried here. The vast high plains are restless. Something about the wind here gives me the idea that the spirits of the dead are compelled to move on.

• • •

Our history is long enough, and our ties to our home are strong enough, to keep many of us anchored to and invested in our state for the long haul. There are problems everywhere in the world for GLBT people, but in Colorado, all some of us have to do is walk outside in order to see, hear, and feel the reasons behind our love of the state. But as binding as the land can be, it's usually secondary to that other tie that binds, although not as legally as some of us would like—love, glorious love, in all its incarnations.

Part Three

Our Loves

In their arguments against GLBT civil rights and their "love the sinner, hate the sin" proclamations, many anti-GLBT conservatives (who, in reality, usually either hate the "sinner" and hate the "sin" or hate the "sinner" and love the "sin") often claim that heterosexuals don't flaunt their sexuality, but that gay men and lesbian women do. In fact, heterosexuality is flaunted every day in every way in our culture. Anytime a straight person says "my husband" or "my wife," that person is flaunting his or her sexuality. Whenever a straight man and woman walk down the street holding hands or steal a kiss at the stoplight, they are flaunting their sexuality. Almost every mainstream movie, television show, book, song, and theatrical production ever produced flaunts heterosexuality. Every engagement or wedding announcement in the newspaper, every spouse or family photograph on a desk at work, every Valentine's Day store display flaunts heterosexuality.

GLBT people live in a world where they are exposed to blatant heterosexuality every day. Straight people live in a world where they can almost always choose whether or not they wish to be exposed to homosexuality. Same-sex couples rarely "flaunt" their sexuality—at least not if they want to stay alive. There are very few places where same-sex couples can feel comfortable even holding hands.

Even so, it's not surprising that many of Colorado's GLBT authors choose to write about relationships. Given the fact that same-sex relationships are not only legally unrecognized in the state but also intentionally sabotaged, it's a wonder that any same-sex couples are able to get together, let alone stay together, at all. The fact that they do—and the fact that gay-, lesbian-, and queer-identified people continue to search for, and find, lasting love in the face of blatant inequality—is a testament to the strength and stability of same-sex relationships.

One of the most loved—and most worn-out—arguments used by Colorado conservatives to oppose same-sex marriage is that allowing it will undermine, and even destroy, heterosexual marriage. Funny, then, how El Paso County, home of Colorado Springs and the center of Evangelical Christian conservatism, has one of the highest divorce rates in the state, according to 2000–2004 statistics from the Colorado Public Health and

Environment office. Same-sex marriage isn't legal in Colorado. Never has been. So who is destroying all those straight marriages?

It's unlikely that it has anything to do with the thousands of GLBT people who live and work in El Paso County and love it there. And it's probably not the many happy same-sex couples who participate in the marriage ceremony held at the Colorado Springs PrideFest—including those who return every year to renew their vows. In fact, as this is being written, the lowest divorce rate in the United States belongs to the state of Massachusetts—the only state in the country at this time with legal same-sex marriage. One thing's for sure—it's not love, of any kind, that's hurting heterosexual marriages.

But we'll let them figure out their own problems. We're too busy looking for love in all the wrong—and sometimes all the right—places. And, with apologies to John Paul Jones, we have not yet begun to flaunt.

Finding It

With the state's large and growing queer population, there are plenty of potential partners from which to choose and plenty of places to go in which to find them. There are at least 50 churches in the Denver metro area alone that are open and affirming, welcoming GLBT members to their congregations. The social and support groups that are available throughout the state provide countless opportunities to meet partners with similar interests and concerns. Political organizations are perfect for the activist, and nonprofit volunteerism is a great way to meet like-minded souls. And then, of course, there are the mainstays of partner procurement for both the GLBT and the straight communities: the personal ads and the bars.

SWGMB, Used

DONALD STIKELEATHER

Donald Stikeleather is a nationally produced choreographer, originally from Cincinnati, who left performing and teaching college to study hospital chaplaincy. His writing first appeared in his own performance work, most notably at the Cleveland Performance Art Festival and recently in the diversity journal Tendrel. *He is currently finishing his Master of Divinity at Naropa University in Boulder and serves as a Senior Writing Fellow at the Naropa Writing Center.*

Trained
Domestic
Handy
Sexually versatile
Drug free
Disease free
Nine years of college
Healthy endowment and healthy liver
Heart already broken
Able to hike long distances
Flatirons or Sanitas
Trained to bike in affluent traffic
Able to process your problems with ease
Good grief listener
Romantic
Will not run out at first sign of adversity
Ballet butt
Social smoker only

Income-producing potential!
Classic find, one of the few queer men of the Reagan era
*   that is still alive*
And only one year in Boulder
Discounts for dents and damage—tonight only
At fifth sign of adversity, he will stop calling
But he is able to recite monologues from the American Theatre
Lack of commitment
But, tonight only, he will show off with you on the dance floor
Over 100,000 miles, but he still smells new
Discount for short erection time (take breaks!)
Loaded—with songs upon request
Naropa Buddhist
He will never say he can't live without you
You could still just have a good time
Ornery and overwhelmed, but with a dry sense of humor
Bisexual, but he has lots of stories
Lack of hair and abundance of extra hair (open to shaving)
No warranty, but lives in the moment
Cash advances from his student loan debit card
Chronic tear duct leak (add water)
Picks nose when alone and sometimes forgets
Damaged goods
What a deal!

•   •   •

Trapped in the Looking Glass

RICHARD McCOMB

Richard McComb is 58 years old and was born in a small town in Illinois. He moved to Colorado in 1972. He has a degree in history and is close to a master's degree with high school teaching credentials, and he has worked as a truck driver and for a magazine and book distributor. He came out as gay at the age of 38, and was assaulted, beaten, and left for dead in 1993. The perpetrators were arrested and sent to prison, and he subsequently returned to an old hobby, painting, and took up writing, using it to explore his spirituality by composing poetry and free verse. He has been coping with several major illnesses and considers himself a survivor trying to better himself. He is single and his interests include writing, painting, history, geology, archaeology, movies, cooking, astronomy, gardening, camping, hiking, and sports. He has traveled extensively in the United States, is a big Civil War buff, and hopes to eventually see Charleston, Savannah, and New England in the fall.

Bright lights, high energy dance floor
Bodies in motion, and so much more
Searching eyes, parting glances
He sure looks good when he dances
Leather, sequins, Levi's, boots and sweat
Smoke-filled rooms, liquor strong and wet
Black curly hair and locks tinted gold
Poking, groping, drugs bought and sold
Men flexing in poses that invite delight
Pretty boys with attitude, looking for Mr. Right

Queens, aglitter, hold court over there
Strange looks, laughter, enticing stare
Gossip, backstabbing, an occasional fight
Music and partying till the wee hours of night
Amidst this sea of flesh, I hope he's here
The face that I've been seeking, I feel is near
It's last call, time is running out real quick
Now they all look alike, I feel a little sick
As I stumble out the door, a hand grabs my wrist
It's the face I was looking for and almost missed
Morning brings a splitting head as I turn to find
The guy I thought must be the one was all just in my mind

• • •

Untangling
the U-Haul Theory

AIMEE HERMAN

Aimee Herman has been described as Woody Allen with a vagina. *No subject is too risqué for her to write about, and she enjoys the challenge of creating a small disturbance on the page. She currently has two chapbooks of poetry published* (Tastes Like Cheesecake *and* If These Thighs Could Talk, *available for purchase by e-mailing her at writerslashpoet@aol.com). Also, check out her spoken word CD,* performance anxiety, *available through www.cdbaby.com/AimeeHerman.*

IT GOES A LITTLE SOMETHING LIKE THIS:

First date. Two lesbians sit across from one another, wrapped within the tightened grasp of intense conversation. No topic is left untouched: children, previous partners, favorite side of the bed coupled with preferred sexual position. It is a candlelit interview minus the w-2 form and 401(K) options.

We do this all the time, rushing past foreplay, skipping traditional flirting and witty banter. We dig toward the important questions, getting to the heart and mind of the woman we hope to spend the rest of our life with, even after just one date.

And when I say *we*, I mean every other lesbian *but* me.

One kiss leads to a little under-the-shirt action. Shirt comes off. Then bra. Pants. Underwear. Socks last. You are having sleepover parties without the hair braiding and nail painting. She forgets an article of clothing at your apartment. Buys an extra toothbrush for you and leaves it in her bathroom. Starts filling her refrigerator with your favorite things to eat, and before you know it, you're hooked.

She begins to receive mail at your address. You have no idea how this happened, but even telemarketers are calling and asking for her. Your life is no longer just yours. It is consumed by her scent and the random hairs you find on your bed, which used to be charming and now seem almost creepy. Even your vagina, your loyal and trusted best friend, has betrayed you, because now even your cycles are the same.

Alas, I rebel! I padlock my door, my medicine cabinet, spread out my long limbs, taking up every inch of the bed, and silence my stubborn vagina.

I will not give in to the U-Haul-lesbian philosophy. I don't even own luggage. Won't invest in it. Refuse to.

I am not the typical lesbian. Love is like milk to me, and I have a major case of lactose-intolerance. When I don't have it, I crave it—tasting it on my tongue and reminiscing about the many times I savored it. But when I get a chance to relish its existence, I no longer want it. My stomach turns and I feel nauseous. I run, purging its toxicity from my system.

I refuse to settle. Why rush? I'm perfectly fine with being alone. I have no qualms about taking myself to a movie or out to dinner. Who needs conversation when your mouth is stuffed with delicious food?

I know what's out there—those one-night stands, when you've had a bit too much to drink and that slightly overweight Jamaican girl you've been playing pool with at the local gay bar suddenly looks good to you. So you give her your phone number. I mean, really give it to her—not some random grouping of numbers that sounds like it could be a location where you might be reached, but your real phone number—though you never expect her to call.

And when I say you, I mean *me*.

And then she calls about a week later, when you have completely forgotten even giving out your number, and you are too embarrassed to ask: *who are you again?* Then it comes back to you. Ladies' night. Three rum and cokes chased with two beers and possibly a shot or two of something silly, like a red-headed-slut or rocky-mountain-mother-fucker, the name of the drink a description of how you feel after you've had a few. You remember that she cornered you in the bathroom and kissed you, her tongue trying to push its way past your tightly sealed lips. She grabbed your ass right before your flustered self gave her your number.

Why are we so impatient? I've been to several gay pride parades. There are plenty of lesbians to go around. We aren't amidst some shortage, where we need to claim the first dyke we see. Lesbians are not like parking spaces. They don't just run out.

So put away your luggage and savor a second helping of foreplay. It's not overrated. It is often forgotten. And although she may be *the one*, there is nothing wrong with making her wait.

• • •

Sometimes finding it is easy. Other times, it can be a little more challenging. We might feel like giving up, or we might go off in another direction entirely before we come back to where we should have been all along. It's not that we're confused about who we are or what we want—it's just that we're living in a culture that does not always support, let alone encourage, those very things. Left to our own devices, we will do quite nicely and come around to our own happy endings.

I Love You Still

FREDERICK LYLE MORRIS

Frederick Lyle Morris has been writing and painting since the age of 11.
He has exhibited his art and writings in Paris, Germany, Asia, and on the
East Coast of the United States. He loves to share his work and touch
others with the joy of expression. He is currently stationed at Fort
Carson, takes writing holidays at his farm in West Virginia, and tours
Europe once a year.

Yesterday, I stood on the banks of forever
looking out over an empty sea. The mist
and haze made seeing tomorrow impossible.
In my sadness, I'd forgotten about
those around me. My pain was so great, I too had
faded from life. Without notice, a light
flickered in the darkness, and I came alive
again. Guarded and chaste, I never gave myself
freely to any man, and when I was willing,
it was too late. Without warning, you kissed
me on the lips, pulled me close, and forced
life into this empty void. Does he love
me, can I love him, is it okay; Words,
thoughts, confusion. Then, in a dream, a
voice so tender whispered, "It's time, you've
cried enough, let me go." As the tears filled
my eyes, I knew. And then it was gone, lifted.
I took a breath, thought of you. Inside,
everything burned. I love you, and all of a
sudden I knew . . . everything would be okay.

• • •

Indebted to Her:
One Kiss in Colorado

KIMBERLEE A. MILLER

Kim Miller *was born and raised in western Massachusetts. She came west in 1984 to attend the University of Colorado, Boulder, where she studied journalism and computer science. Colorado's mountains quickly became a passion for her and she made her home here and has never left. It took her more than three decades to discover that she was gay. She works full-time as an application developer for the county government. She has two children, ages 13 and 18. She has written four full-length screenplays and writes articles and poetry as often as time permits. She plays competitive women's ice hockey, runs, hikes, bikes, and climbs.*

Kim has recently been published in The Forum Magazine *and online at www.archronicles.com/8003.htm. She is currently searching for subject matter that will help her achieve a high level of literary notoriety and that will help increase the depth of her pockets.*

Thirty three years
of cheap aftershave,
whiskers,
and grunting atop me.
I prefer
to forget
the days I struggled
to walk crookedly
down that straight line
. . . and to remember
when she told me
to wipe

her lipstick
from my lips
after that first kiss.
I've heard from others
like me
the same thing . . .
. . . one kiss
it took
to turn their
insides out,
to make them step back
and re-evaluate
every feeling
they'd ever felt.
And now
when my little fingers
slide slowly
down
to explore
that salty softness,
I have to close
my eyes
to catch
my breath.
I guess in the end
it doesn't matter
that it took
so long
to realize
that intimacy
can also be
a glance . . .
a conversation . . .
two hands pressed

gently together.
It matters only
that now
I'm able to
skip contently
over top that
straight line
as crookedly as
I please,
laughing . . .
at its insignificance.

●   ●   ●

How Did I Get Here?

SHAKIRAH C. HEMSTROM

*Shakirah C. Hemstrom lives with her partner, Cathy, in Ault, Colorado.
She was born and raised on a farm near Olathe, Colorado, and raised her
four kids as a single mom in Gunnison, Colorado. She changed her given
name from Gail to her adult name, Shakirah, in 1998 as a result of a
spiritual experience. She has her hands in many pots, including a private
counseling practice.*

I LOOKED IN THE MIRROR at the red handprint on my naked
white bun cheek.

"Ouch. Why'd you do that?"

"Oh, it looks so pretty," Cath said as she slapped my other cheek.
I took it happily and wondered why.

How did I get here anyway? I thought to myself. I had lately been
having the strange sensation that I was waking from a long dream.
Looking around me, I realized how different things were from a year
and a half ago. Back then, I was successfully running my own counseling practice and living alone in my hometown, where I had raised
my four kids. Back then, I had no idea that most people would have
called me a lesbian.

It's true that Stephanie and I did sleep together—there were too
many kids around to do anything *but* sleep—but I assumed that, since
I had not made an advance, I was not a lesbian. Sure, I had always
been a little dykey in appearance, and friends had told me so. But that
didn't make me a lesbian, did it?

And when Stephanie invited her new beau, Alfonzo—not me—to
spend Christmas Eve with her and her kids, well, I left her with a
thing or two to think about. But that didn't make me a lesbian—did

it? She didn't call after that, though I sat by the phone waiting for an apology. Oh, well. It was only a friendship.

I spent most of the following month in bed. And that's when I decided to find a girlfriend. And that *did* make me a lesbian. *I'll worry about consequences later*, I thought as I signed up for an Internet dating membership.

Within three days I had an e-mail from Cath. She wanted to meet me. I wanted more than to meet her. I wanted a rescue. I wanted love. I wanted a girlfriend I could call my own. I wanted to leave town, move to a new place, find a new life—and I got what I wanted. Within four months, I was moved in, 300 miles from the place I called home.

I had fallen in love—and fallen hard. Since then, things have been muddy. In fact, I'm not sure who I am anymore.

I have a new practice that doesn't make any money, a new hometown where I have no roots, and a cell phone to keep tabs with my adult children—a poor substitute for being there. But I stay. I stay and stay and stay.

Have I let my sexual needs determine everything for me? For the past year and a half I've been able to think of nothing but being with Cath. Now I'm wondering if I have given up too much for sex. Am I just a greedy sex fanatic? Am I perpetuating a lesbian stereotype?

When I told Cath that I was writing a story about us, she asked me, "So what, do you want me to come over there and give you something to write about?"

"Well, that depends on what you mean," I said.

"How about something like this?"

She moved me over to the kitchen sink and leaned me against it, gently probing with the sweet, kind hand that I love so much. I wanted her; she knew it. Orgasm wracked my body. If this makes me a greedy sex fanatic, I thought, bring it on. Heck, even if it perpetuates a lesbian stereotype—bring it on.

She licked her fingers and went back to her drawing, and I wobbled, weak-kneed, to make some tea. She's an artist and somewhat of a rebel. I'm a flaming lesbian—and having the time of my life.

• • •

Keeping It

Once we've found the one we want—or the one we think we want—then we have the little task of keeping that person entertained, enchanted, beguiled, and amused. Gone are the days when gay men placed furtive ads for friendship in the classified section of bodybuilding magazines, and the only requirement for a potential partner was that he live in the same state. Now that we're out and aware of our numbers, with high-tech tools that allow us to communicate across cities, states, and even countries, we can afford to be a little more choosy and a little more invested in our choices. But these freedoms also make the competition fierce, and holding on to someone can be difficult at best.

Colorado's increasing GLBT population can mean a lot of newcomers, and thus a lot of excitement for those out in the dating pool. It can also mean swimming upstream, trying not to let the big one—or even the small one—get away.

Size Matters

DAN STONE

Dan Stone is a freelance journalist, poet, essayist, and novelist. His work has appeared in White Crane Journal; A&U Magazine; Astropoetica; Bay Windows; Chiron Review; Queer Poets Journal; Brave New Tick; Charmed Lives: Gay Spirit in Storytelling; Gents, Bad Boys, and Barbarians: New Gay Male Poetry; *and* Rebel Yell: Stories by Contemporary Southern Gay Authors. *He currently lives in the Denver area, and can be reached via e-mail at dan@dansville.net or at www.successalliances.com.*

AGAZINES AND CATALOGS have always been a means of escape for me. I can never keep track of exactly how many subscriptions I have going. I know I get both *Time* and *Newsweek*—for balanced coverage of world events—*Life, National Geographic, The Smithsonian, Better Homes and Gardens* and *5280*. I subscribe to several gay ones, of course—*Genre, Men's Style, Advocate Men*. My favorites are the health and fitness mags—*Men's Health, Men's Fitness, Exercise for Men Only*—and, of course, the catalogs.

I've been on the mailing list for *International Male* and *Undergear* for at least seven or eight years—ever since I moved my tiny life out of Wyoming and into the large, dry lake of Denver. I like *IM* and *Undergear* not so much because of the clothes—I've ordered two things in eight years that I'd ever wear out of the house—but, big surprise, because of the men.

I've had lots of favorite models over the years, but when I saw Dominic, I forgot about all of them—and anyone else I'd ever laid eyes on. He was the *IM* summer cover—a glorious full-length shot of him on the beach wearing item M845, the new Super Nova bikini in royal blue. He was better than gorgeous. He was lean and he looked a little pissed off, even though he was grinning like he'd just tripped the photographer. He had close-cropped, dark brown hair, wicked eyes—and chest hair. As his profile made very clear, this guy was no Valley Boy:

"Dominic Santini brings his Italian good looks to L.A. by way of Brooklyn, where he developed his 6', 170-lb physique in the boxing ring at Manny's gym. When he's not in front of the camera, he's back in the gym or on his bike—or in the kitchen making his mom's homemade spaghetti. He can still throw a wicked punch."

I'd never cut out anyone's picture before. Swear to God. But I knew I had to have Dominic Santini. I didn't stop with the cover. As was often the case with new *IM* models, he was practically on every other page. He looked as good in the textured, sandwashed, three-piece silk suit as he did in the Tactics thong. Of course, they had to show him in the gym, in their hot new triple-stripe unitard. And I must say, he packed quite a pouch in the Foreign Legion gauze brief, though I would have preferred to see him in navy rather than ivory. He could even get away with wearing those tacky trail-tracker sandals. Dominic Santini had handsome feet.

I don't know that I would call it an obsession. I put up the pictures of Dominic because they made me happy. When he looked over his shoulder at me from the bulletin board over my computer, he inspired me. When he smiled sweetly from the refrigerator door, I felt warmed and somehow less hungry. And when he looked up at me, half imp and half angel, from the nightstand beside my bed, I would have such dreams . . .

YOU WOULD THINK that I'd remember the exact date and time that he hopped down from the bulletin board onto my desk. It's not the sort of thing that normally happens here. But what I do remember vividly is coming back from the kitchen to find Dominic sitting with one leg over the side of the desk, resting an elbow on the other knee, waiting patiently for me to return with my third cup of coffee, which immediately dropped straight out of my hand onto the carpet.

He said, "Jesus, buddy, you better get a cold washcloth before that stain sets. Or better yet, get some club soda!" Actually, he said in thick Brooklynese, "Jesus, buddy, you bedduh get a cold washclueth buhfooer that stain sets. Oouh bedduh yet, get some club soda!"

I didn't move. I didn't blink.

"Move it!" he snapped. "You gonna ruin your carpet!"

It was a great icebreaker. By the time I got the stain neutralized— under Dominic's supervision—it seemed kind of rude to turn around and ask, *So how the fuck did you get from being a catalog cutout to a pint-sized hunk sitting here talking to me on top of my desk?*

"My uncle owns a carpet store in Brooklyn," he said when I thanked him for the emergency rug-saving technique. "I used to work for him in the summers when I was in school."

I didn't say "Yeah? Was your uncle lean, mean, and ten inches tall, too?" I think the reason I kept my mouth shut was, first of all, it seemed too weird for words. And second, it was starting to hit me. Dominic Santini was there on my desk. He was real. He was talking to me. And he was even sweeter looking in the flesh, even sexier in three dimensions.

Under different circumstances I might have questioned him more. I might have demanded some explanation for his appearing like he did out of nowhere. I might have gotten pissed the way you get pissed at God for suddenly answering one of your prayers—but with a sarcastic twist—after ignoring you for years. But none of that mattered. I was already lame-brained in love with Dominic. For months, his face had been the last thing I had seen before going to sleep and the first thing I had seen in the morning. He'd been in my dreams. He'd taken them over. I'd always known he was special. It was clear to me just from the look in his eyes and the way that his smile hit me right between the legs. Dominic was my dream.

"Where did you come from?" I finally asked.

"You want something bad enough and wait long enough, you get it," he said.

I was glad to hear it.

HAVING DOMINIC AROUND changed everything. It changed my whole point of view. I guess I knew somewhere in the back of my mind that it was an unusual relationship. I wasn't blind. He was the size of a catalog cover, for Christ's sake. I didn't care. When I walked into a room and he was there, it was like I'd never been in that room before in my whole life—like it was the room I'd always wanted to walk into.

The first time we did it, it wasn't smooth. I was pretty inexperienced. But Dominic was patient and careful—not rough at all. This fighter had a soul. I don't think that it's important to describe the details, the twists and turns and concessions we had to make to allow our very different bodies to fit. Sure there were some things we couldn't do. But no matter how complete an attraction seems, it's always a series of negotiations and compromises—one person bending or stretching to conform to another. Of searching and finding. And waiting. It was private. And I won't say it was perfect, but it was transforming in the way only something tender can be. Time stood still.

From that moment on, nothing looked or felt the same. For the first time in my little gray halftone of a life, the glass looked half full. Instead of thinking of home as an escape or a retreat, I began to think of it as an adventure. I'd never had so much fun. He would be waiting for me in a different room of my apartment every time I came in. And always in a different outfit. I think he liked dressing up—or down—for me.

I could always tell what mood he was in by what he was wearing when I came through the door. Sometimes he'd dress to the nines in the black gabardine jacket and scissor-pleated pants, with the paisley vest and patent leather slip-ons. Or he'd be lounging around in the sexy, one-piece, cotton jersey step-in. He was so talented, he could switch from the skin-tight, studded leather pants and peekaboo tank top to the embroidered matador jacket and pirate shirt without losing one iota of credibility. I loved these private fashion shows. It was like coming home to a different person every night. It gave me something to look forward to.

I would lie awake sometimes and watch him curled up and asleep on the pillow next to me. Now and then he would wake up, as if he knew even when he was sleeping that I was awake, that I wanted to talk to him.

"Why you not asleep?" he'd say.

"What if I go to sleep and wake up and you're not here?" I asked. "What if I find out you're really a dream?"

He smiled my favorite smile. "What do you do when you have a really good dream that you don't wanna forget?"

I had to think about that. "Sometimes I write it down," I said. It was true. I kept sort of a journal—not an everyday thing, but whenever something came along that I thought I should remember. There were a few dreams in there, although most of them had been kind of unpleasant, like warnings I should heed.

"Well, if you ever wake up and I'm not here beside you, baby doll, then write it down. Think of me as a good dream you'll want to remember."

When Dominic called me baby doll, nothing else mattered. I rose like a falcon over the Rockies. I was just too happy to . . . sweat the small stuff.

I DON'T KNOW WHEN things started to change. I really lost track of dates there for a while. I guess the first indication I had was one afternoon on the light rail. For the first time since Dominic had shown up, I caught myself looking at another man. Really looking. There was nothing all that striking about him. Medium brown hair. Nice eyes. Ordinary-looking clothes. Average height. I couldn't take my eyes off him.

I had put up Dominic's picture in a discreet corner of my cubicle at work. It went unnoticed for weeks, perhaps months, but one day Samuel Willoughby, this bitchy queen from Boulder who works in payroll, saw the photo when he stopped by to drop off my check. Samuel was the only person in the entire company who ever once set foot inside my cube.

"Who's he?" he asked, looking at Dominic's picture.

"A friend."

Samuel looked skeptical. "How tall is he?" Coming from anyone else this would have been a ridiculous question. He had an infuriating way of asking the one thing you hoped no one would ask.

"Gee, I never took a tape measure to him," I said, imagining Samuel burning in hell.

"Hmm. He looks . . . short."

It shouldn't have bothered me. Nothing Samuel said had ever mattered to me before. As a psychoanalyst might say, however, this was merely a symptom. For a while, I thought it was just me, just some pesky malaise that would pass like most of my moods. I had no idea that Dominic was being affected as well, until I came home from work one afternoon and he was nowhere to be found.

At first, I thought he was just playing hide-and-seek. I looked under pillows and in wastebaskets. I opened drawers. Finally, I just walked from room to room with a sinking sensation in my stomach, saying, "Oh, Dominic, oh, Dominic," over and over.

"I'm in here," I finally heard a muffled voice say. It was coming from my bedroom, but when I'd walked back into the room, still no Dominic.

"Dominic?" I said, lifting the lid to the clothes hamper.

"In here."

This time, the voice was clearly coming from the very large, ornately carved, mahogany music box I kept on top of the dresser. It was an unusually large music box that also served as a jewelry box, with carved doors that swung open in the front. It had been my mother's since she was a girl and was one of the few things I had that belonged to her. I'd been fascinated by it as a child, because whenever the doors were opened, a very small-boned, fragile-looking, carved ballerina in white lace would begin to pirouette on a tiny platform to music from *The Nutcracker*. There was no telling how many hours I'd spent opening and closing the doors to that music box before the poor, worn-out ballerina finally refused to dance another step.

I slowly opened the door to the music box, and there sat Dominic.

"What are you doing in there?" I asked.

There were mirrors on the back of each mahogany door, and Dominic was staring at the reflection of himself alongside the ballerina. He was quiet for a long time. "We're about the same height," he finally said.

"What are you doing in there?" I repeated.

Dominic would not look at me. "I thought I might be able to fix her. I used to be pretty good at fixing things."

"It's all right," I said. "She hasn't worked for years. Don't worry about it."

"No," he said. "I *wanted* to fix her." There was an impatient edge in his voice. Or was it more like sorrow? "I thought that if I could get her to work, I'd have someone who could dance with me."

I had nothing to say to that. I couldn't help thinking that I was somehow responsible for making him feel small.

The next day at work, I called *International Male*'s twenty-four-hour customer service number to see if there was a life-size poster available of Dominic Santini, thinking, with a lunatic's logic, that maybe he could sort of reinvent himself, like leaving the room and coming back in with a different point of view. The service rep said there was no poster, and he asked politely if I'd like for him to send me the summer catalog with Dominic on the cover.

"You don't understand how important this is," I said.

The service rep said he was sorry.

I never told Dominic that I'd called about the poster. How do you tell someone you love that there's something about him, something he has no hope of changing, that is becoming impossible to live with? How do you put something so awful into words? All I could think of to say was how great he looked. I started telling him every chance I got. Every time I came home and found him waiting. Every time he changed outfits. Every morning when I woke up with him on the pillow beside me.

"Good morning, Handsome," I'd say. It was like a secret code. I thought only I knew what it meant. He certainly never let me see that he was catching on. We played the same games. We followed the same routine. I don't even know how much time had passed when I came home from work one evening and found that he was gone. I don't mean that I couldn't find him. I looked for him. I called out his name, but the whole time I knew he was gone for good. Sometimes you just know.

For the first couple of days, I wandered around from room to room, trying to remember everything that had happened. It seemed important—and the least I could do for Dominic—to miss him as much as possible. When I finally forced myself to gather up all his pictures, I thought that no one would ever believe that a guy like Dominic had come to life for me. I still had trouble believing it myself. How could I explain his coming or his going?

"You want something bad enough and wait long enough, you get it," he had said.

"And when you get it, you forget how bad you wanted it," I said to myself as I looked through all his pictures, through Dominic's many poses, all so sexy and beautiful. Eventually I put away all the pictures and magazines in a box in the attic, except for the one of Dominic on the beach—the one in the royal blue Super Nova bikini.

Growth is a pretty relative thing, but I couldn't help feeling that maybe I'd inched up at least a fraction, and all thanks to Dominic. I looked at his sweet face, feeling mostly like the little shit that I'd been, but also realizing that, for once, I'd had an opportunity to really be the bigger guy. Even though I'd blown it, I'd had a shot at something larger than my puny life. Maybe I'd get another chance and manage not to cock it up this time.

"If you ever wake up and I'm not here beside you, baby doll, then write it down. Think of me as a good dream you'll want to remember."

Maybe putting our story on paper was too little, too late, but it was the best I could do to give Dominic some of the credit he deserved. I got out the old Italian leather-bound book with the authentic unlined parchment paper that I'd bought at Barnes & Noble and the ruby red Cross pen that I used only for recording my most private thoughts.

Before starting to write, I picked up Dominic's picture and held it in my very average-sized hands. The guy may not have been quite as big as my dreams, but damn if the camera didn't love him.

• • •

Escape

TIGRE HALLER

*Originally from New York, where he hosted performance salons and created interactive theatrical pieces, **Tigre Haller** has been involved with the arts for many years. Tigre moved to Denver nine years ago with his partner and has recently completed writing his first volume of poetry,* Left of Divine, *and is near completion of a play,* #44. *His poems have been published in independent zines and in the Web anthology* Voices in Wartime.

He was a nominee for the PEN America/Newman's Own First Amendment award for his organization of Banned Books Read Outs, which educated the public on present-day censorship issues while celebrating our freedom to read and freedom of speech. This work was done in partnership with the Rocky Mountain Book Festival. Tigre also served as Membership Chair for the Colorado Independent Publishers Association. Most recently, Tigre volunteered for the "Yes on I" campaign to achieve basic rights for same-sex couples in Colorado. He is honored to be included as part of this inaugural publication.

I want to escape into you
Out of the blistering cold of this Denver morning
This place was never so frigid as it has become
Childhood has dried up in the frost
Withered my bones and left me with no insulation

I want to escape into you
Lick your wounds and meld with
Eccentric joy
Listen to your laughter in my dreams
And retrace the steps of a happier life

           I want to escape into you
Don't question my motivation
Only know that now—this moment—
I am yours completely
As if I ever belonged to anyone else

Your quirks are salve for a heart
Weary of mere simulation, yet
Stimulated by your caress
Affection more blissful than
The mechanics of sex
           I want to escape into you

Trust my sincerity even if
Ecstasy might not last
I want to escape into you
So that I no longer will be
        Alone

• • •

Secretly, as Certain Dark Things Are Loved

CHRISTOPHER CALDWELL

Christopher Caldwell is a California expatriate who is still alternately baffled and amazed by Colorado. He works in Jefferson County as a counselor for at-risk youth, who never fail to teach him something new about the human condition. He has been published in Oasis, Metromode, *and* SNiPe; *was a frequent contributor and content editor for the writing site www.everything2.com; and wrote a hilariously failed advice column under the pseudonym Madam Lean. He does enjoy walks on the beach and candlelight dinners, but will not be offended if you don't.*

BETTER," HE SAYS as he buttons the fly on his pre-faded jeans and stares at the vertical blinds covering my window. "There's no attachments this way. No jealousy, none of that bullshit."

He makes eye contact and I smile mysteriously and focus my gaze on the tattoo on his upper right arm. It's a Dao, with flames above it and ice below, but the green and blue crystals of ice resemble a wing in the half-light; briefly I fantasize about flying away. He pulls me toward him and kisses me, hard and sudden. I pull away and gasp for air and turn my head.

"You're going to be late," I say, glancing down at the little moons at the base of my fingernails. He grunts something and fumbles around, looking for his shirt.

He tousles my hair, a gesture I find somehow condescending. He does not look back as he walks toward the door. "Better," I whisper at his shadow.

I decide to go out. I stare at my own reflection in the mirror and take stock: unruly black hair, skin the brown of Spanish onions, dark eyes. There is a purpling bruise at the place where my neck meets my shoulder. There are teethmarks near my nipple. For someone who values no attachment and no jealousies, he is entirely too fond of leaving marks. He marks his territory. My eyes have a cruel cast to them. I need a shave.

Showered and shaved, love bites hidden beneath a collared shirt, I hit the streets. I am looking for the opposite of the friendly neighborhood bar. Someplace dark and quiet and smoky. Someplace where I can be lost. It's three in the afternoon. A good time to find bars that cater to serious drinking and not entertaining.

I find a dive next to a paint store. It looks like the right kind of place. No windows, a neon sign above the door in old-fashioned looping letters. I imagine the lurid red glow of the sign at night. I imagine that the "C" does not light up. I push open the front door. The walls are paneled in wood, there's a circular firepit in the center of the room, and a dour, grey-haired woman with meaty arms stands behind the bar. She nods at me as I approach. The barstool I sit on has had its seat patched over several times with duct tape, the original burgundy color almost hidden beneath gummy silver. I think I should order something ballsy and masculine like a double scotch on the rocks, but instead ask for a Cuba libre. She nods, then splashes rum into a glass without measuring, spritzes in Coke from the tap, and adds a lime and two swizzle sticks. She hands it to me on a slightly damp napkin.

The drink is surprisingly strong, and I knock it back quickly, feeling the warmth in my chest. There are packets of airline peanuts in a small wooden bowl on the bar, their foil wrappers gone slightly dusty with neglect. I take one. While attempting to open it, I pull too hard and spill peanuts and honey-roast salt over the counter. I trace his name in the salt before sweeping it all away with my napkin. The bartender hasn't said a word to me, and I find this comforting. No comments on my drinking this early in the day, nothing about my eyes looking sad. Her face is blank, a wall of cinderblock I feel free to decorate with mental graffiti. I order another drink. Scanning the room, I see an old-fashioned cigarette vending machine, the kind with the knobs and levers. Perversely, I think about buying a pack and lighting up. I don't smoke. Instead, I finish my second drink, pay my bill and leave.

I go for a walk. There's a summer wind, gritty and humid, and the jacaranda trees that jut up from the sidewalk sway and shower me with blossoms. On the horizon, there's the threat of a thunderstorm. The blue blossoms that carpet the pavement bleed into purple as they're crushed beneath my feet. Both aimless and restless, I walk along the street, staring into storefronts. I pass a little Pentecostal church that was a used bookstore six months before. I can hear the rattle of a tambourine, the low moan of an electric organ. I stare into the window and see a heavy middle-aged woman dressed in white dancing, twirling with wild abandon, a paper fan in her hand. There is a savage joy on her face. She closes her eyes against the world as she twirls. The other people in the tiny church raise their hands above their heads and shout, "Glory! Hallelujah!" Weary and poor, they reach toward salvation and perfect love. The minister singsongs something I can barely hear, and the heavy woman appears to faint. For a long time, I stand and watch through the window until the first drops of rain fall. No one sees me staring, no one invites me in out of the rain. I do not own an umbrella and decide to go home.

The clouds have turned my house comfortably dark, and the rain beats against my windows. I turn on music and look through my bookshelves for something to read. It's Thursday. His art class is three hours long—more than two have passed. He likes to come over again on Thursday evenings. The afternoon quickie will have only whet his singular appetite and he will arrive after class ends and fall upon me with kisses and bites as if I were an expensive morsel of dark chocolate.

Maybe I shouldn't be at home when he returns. No attachments means that I, too, can be unavailable. Perhaps I will go out and meet someone new. Someone who will read Neruda to me, and whose puppylike devotion I will eventually despise. Perhaps I will just lie here in the darkness and pretend I am gone when he returns. "Better," I say to myself.

But when the knock at my front door comes, I get up and open it and let him in.

• • •

Losing It

Sometimes they do get away—and sometimes we let them go. Although our visibility and our numbers create the stress of more competition, these very same factors allow us the freedom to walk away rather than remain in an unhappy or dysfunctional relationship because we fear that we may never find another.

There is the argument that, if we were allowed to legally marry, our commitments might be more carefully considered, our endings delayed as we worked toward resolution rather than dissolution. It's a valid position, and one that should be taken into consideration by the powers-that-will-never-let-us-be.

But there are GLBT couples in Colorado who have been together for decades and who have made it a point to let those powers know—by testifying at the state legislature in favor of domestic partnerships, two-parent-same-sex-couple adoptions, and other pro-GLBT legislation. They have stayed together in spite of, not because of, the current policies on legal protection and support for same-sex couples.

So for those who are looking for love, even a breakup doesn't have to be the end of the road. There are plenty more where that one came from, and there are plenty of role models out there to let us know that, if we want a long-term relationship, it certainly can be had. And if we don't? Well, that option is always available as well. Hills and valleys—that's what Colorado's made of.

He Said, I Said

David Alan

*David Alan was born in Alabama, but overcame that obstacle. He is a
military brat and has lived all across this country. He is a military veteran
himself, having driven a tank in Germany in the early '80s. He came to
Colorado in March 1997 and has been involved in the community since
that time. He has had one wife and two-and-a-half husbands. He is
currently single. He has been out since approximately 1981, and is glad
for the opportunity to share his story.*

"I WANT TO GO TO THAILAND for a month," he says. "I want
to charter a boat and go scuba diving with my friends." He
doesn't say, "Would you like to go to Thailand with me?" He
doesn't say, "Can you take a month away from work?"

I say, "That sounds like quite the adventure." I say, "Fall is my favorite season." I don't say, "Why do you want to torture me with
your behavior?" I don't say, "I hate you for making me feel this way."

He snuggles very well in his bed with me. I forget about Thailand
for now. When I arrived at his home earlier tonight, he was all smiles
and promises. Where did that man go? Or am I the one who changed?

DONALD IS THE KIND OF MAN who could make you believe just
about anything. His clear pale eyes are like the sea at dawn after a stormy
night, and his hair, all swept forward to frame his face, makes him look
like one of the heroes of the Revolutionary War. The gray looks so distin-
guished. He has a laugh that makes me want to laugh along. And oh,
those eyes. When I first met him, it was a challenge not to stutter while
looking at his face. I thought that I had finally met someone who could
keep me on my toes—or go toe to toe with me.

Now I curse him for making me think that I could get involved with a man again. We haven't seen each other in over a week, and he's left me a message on the machine. I think he misses me.

His family has been in town to see him. He says, "My mother is dying." He says, "I'm upset and think I should take my medicine." He doesn't say, "I need you." He doesn't say, "Please, come to me."

I say, "I'm sorry to hear about your mother. Please give her my best." I say, "Maybe you should call your doctor in the morning." I don't say, "I ache to be with you." I don't say, "I want to hold you and chase all your problems away."

WE MET AT A DANCE CLUB almost three years ago. The second time we ran into each other, I was in his neighborhood and stopped at the local bar for a nightcap. He happened to be there, too. I had no idea I would be seeing Donald. I just wanted one cocktail and then it was off to bed alone for me. I was very surprised when he came up and reintroduced himself, then asked me to come home with him. We sat up and talked for hours. He asked me to make some time for him—for us. I agreed.

About a week later, I called to let him know that I had worked out my schedule to have every other weekend off. I had rearranged my life at his request. His answering machine took the message, and I didn't hear a word from him for over a year.

THERE ARE TIMES when I truly wish I was on my own island and people only came to visit at my invitation. But people find ways to build bridges to your space and then invade. Damn them. Why do people have to be so intoxicating? "Toxic" is an integral part of that word. I'm sure it is not coincidental.

"I want to renew our friendship," he says. "I don't ever want to lose contact again." He doesn't say, "I want you." He doesn't say, "I love you."

I don't say, "I love you." I don't say, "Leave me alone."

"What time do you want me to be there?" I say. "I can be there within the hour."

Over dinner, we have the talk. He asks me why I don't give any input into the ideas he is bringing forth. The silence is almost deafening. I'm stalling for time to think of a grand answer to his question. I finally tell him that I did not realize he was seeking my opinion. I explain that I try not to put my nose where it doesn't belong. I need an express invitation from the interested party. This conversation is the opening to the best dialogue we have ever had. If we had been able to communicate like this at the start, we may have never parted company in the first place.

He assures me that he is interested in what I think. He opens the door and I walk in.

"You are so easy to love," he says. "If you weren't in my life, it would hurt me." He doesn't say, "Please stay with me." He doesn't say, "You are the only one I want."

I can feel my eyes mist up. "I have deep feelings for you, too," I say. "I want to know where you see me fitting in with all of your plans." I don't say, "You are such a bastard." I don't say, "I love you."

We sit at the table after eating for an hour. We discuss our ideal mates. We explain exactly what it is that we want from each other. He tells me that he wants to go very slow with this relationship. He actually calls it a relationship. He cannot even put a name to the kind of relationship we are having. I do ask for his input. I do not want to be too presumptuous.

Eventually we decide to simply say that we are enjoying each other's company. That almost sounds clinical. I realize that it rhymes with cynical. I feel that I have earned that much. Three years of my life, I have the right.

"I'm thinking about buying a different house," he says. "I want something bigger, more formal." He doesn't say, "What part of town would you like to live in?" He doesn't say, "What style do you think you might be most comfortable in?"

He wonders aloud whether or not people might think he is a braggart. I suggest that as long as he keeps his tone sincere and humble, people might not take offense.

"What size house were you thinking of?" I say. "What is wrong with the house you have now?" I don't say, "When are we going to look at property?" I don't say, "When do you want to live together?"

I am thinking that I don't care what kind of house it is as long as he does not hang up those damn pictures of his ex-boyfriends. I concede that he did take them, and they may be very artsy, but I don't want to see them every day. Besides, what would all of my friends think? Why doesn't he ask for pictures of me to hang on his precious walls? Why doesn't he take a few shots of me? I think we should decide on what is in the home as a team.

"I don't think we should live together yet," he says. "I need more time before I can give you that kind of commitment." He doesn't say, "It's over. Leave me alone." He doesn't say, "I need more space. I want more time away from you, from us."

I don't say, "Whatever you want." I don't say, "I am okay with that."

What I *do* say is, "I understand. Goodbye."

• • •

Carousel

SHANNON BULLOCK

Shannon Bullock is from Orange County, California. During her high school years, she moved to Littleton, Colorado, and then ventured to Fort Collins to attend Colorado State University. While there, she completed three degrees in history and political science.

E SIT ACROSS FROM EACH OTHER at IHOP. We had just closed the bar, and she said that she was starving. Both of us order pancakes.

But when the food arrives, she doesn't touch it. She stirs pieces of pancake in the syrup on her plate. She always drenches her pancakes with a ridiculous amount of syrup—not even regular syrup, but the flavored, sugar-packed syrup.

"Baby, what's wrong?" I say. "You've been acting funny for quite some time now."

She shrugs her shoulders.

I reach across the table for her hand, but as soon as my skin touches hers, she recoils. She actually recoils. And I know.

"Who is it?"

Her eyes meet mine briefly, and then she stares at the pancakes again. The disgusting pancakes soaked in red syrup.

"Who in the hell is it?"

"Keep your voice down," she says as she looks up at me again. "What do you want me to say?"

"Tell me the truth."

She laughs. "The truth? What's the point, Allie?"

"I think that I have the right to know. I think that I have the right to hear it from you."

"You already know."

I stare at her, and think that I no longer know her. Suddenly, I am with a complete stranger.

"I have a pretty good idea," I say. "I think I have known for some time. But I still want to hear it from you. Don't you think you at least owe me that, Kristin?"

She takes a deep breath, sets her fork down, fidgets in her chair, and then says, "It's Susan."

Susan. Susan, her best friend. Susan, her married best friend. Susan, her straight, married best friend.

I realize that my life as I know it has just ended at IHOP—an IHOP in the middle of Fort Collins. Shit, why is this happening? The room starts to spin. I look around and try to focus on something, anything so I won't puke. Across the room, I notice a large man shoveling food into his mouth. He's chewing with his mouth open and small chunks of food are falling into his lap. The woman he's with doesn't seem to care or notice.

"You knew our relationship was in trouble," Kristin is saying. "It's not like you did anything to convince me to stay. You didn't try to stop it."

I stare at her for a few seconds, then stutter, "Wh . . . Wh . . . What?"

"Why didn't you stop it?"

I look over again at the fat guy and realize that his image will forever be burned into my memory. Whenever I replay this incident, that man shoveling food into his fucking fat face will be there. That fat guy, chewing like a cow, will be there. *Oh, my god, did he really just put half a cheeseburger into his mouth?*

"I never meant to hurt you," I hear Kristin say. "It's not like we planned for this to happen. It just did . . ."

We. Now my girlfriend and Susan are a "we."

The table next to us is filled with college kids trying to sober up from their night on the town. From the looks of them, they all need a shower. One of the girls makes a mad dash for the bathroom. Obviously, she hasn't learned how to hold her liquor yet.

Oh, she's still talking. Kristin's still talking. Focus, Allie.

"She listens to me. She takes an interest in my life."

Oh, my god, the fat man has ordered dessert. How much food can someone cram into his face? Does this woman not know that he's disgusting? Does he not know it? It's two in the morning, how much food does he need?

I feel like screaming, "Close your mouth, you fat fucking slob."

Kristin has stopped talking and she's staring at me. She knows that I am no longer paying attention. I don't even have the energy to pretend anymore.

"I never meant for any of this to happen," she says.

I look at her. I have nothing to say.

"It's time to get off of the carousel," she says.

I eat my pancakes.

• • •

Our relationships can complement us, complete us, keep us sane, or drive us crazy, but we will never give them up as we carry on the fight for their legal recognition—and in Colorado, we are making headway every day. But even as we continue to work toward full equality for the Colorado GLBT community, we remain individuals, searching out our identity and finding our place within the whole.

PART FOUR

OUR SELVES

Identity can be a precarious thing for anyone—it slips, it slides, and it changes as we move through life, sometimes just taking us along for the ride. But developing a secure and comfortable identity can often be even more challenging for GLBT people. In childhood, when we begin to realize who we are, we also come to realize that who we are is not necessarily who our family, our friends, our society, or even our world wants us to be. So we sometimes expend a lot of energy avoiding our identity, fighting it, trying to change it, or keeping it hidden from everyone else's view.

Unfortunately, this go-along-to-get-along masquerade can sometimes lead to disastrous consequences for ourselves and our loved ones, as we in Colorado have seen firsthand. Personal identity is strong and will not be silenced or hidden away for too long. It slips through the cracks and slides through the crevices that form in any façade, and it finally forces us to change the way we see and feel about ourselves.

Our earliest lessons in our own value and worth come from our family of origin and, later on, from society. Both the Colorado Anti-Violence Program and the National Coalition of Anti-Violence Programs see increases in GLBT hate crimes that often coincide with monumental, and thus controversial, legislation that favors the community, or with the promotion of anti-GLBT policies, such as the Federal Marriage Amendment, and the anti-gay political rhetoric that goes along with it. Those with power and influence who spew vitriolic anti-gay sentiments deny any link between their words and actions and violence against the community, but a look at the statistics proves otherwise—and it's hard to believe that, somewhere under all their disclaimers, they don't already know that.

But when family and some segments of society are not there for us, there are other directions we can head and other paths we can take, knowing that there will be people there to welcome us when we arrive and that we will be stronger for the journey.

Faggot

Alex C. Dembicki

Alex C. Dembicki is a previously unpublished author and poet and a perpetual student of life. A native of Denver, Colorado, Alex currently attends the University of Colorado at Denver as a part-time undergrad in the never-ending pursuit of a degree in the Starving Arts. He works for the Denver Center for the Performing Arts and is a devotee of all things dark, weird, and tattooed, as well as a fierce lover of animals. He is a smart-ass and cynic, button pusher and iconoclast, and believes that religion and politics will be the ultimate destruction of humanity.

THE ATTACK WAS SUDDEN AND BRUTAL, a fervent barrage of boots and fists that sent me sprawling into the earthy scent of recently mowed grass. The vicious beating seemed to last an eternity, yet somehow I managed to walk away with nothing worse than a hairline fracture to my scapula. The deepest wound I sustained in the attack was torn open by one hateful word spit breathlessly over and over: *faggot.* The venomous barbs of that word struck me with more force than the passionate brutality of the boots kicking my face and crushing my chest.

They know. A desperate terror welled up inside me, tasting like the metallic heat of my own blood. *They know and now I'm going to die.* As I flailed helplessly, trying to protect myself from the assault, I noticed several people in the park, no more than twenty feet away, witnessing the attack. They did nothing. *Faggot!*

I had resigned myself to the fact that this would be where and how my life would end when a truck came crashing through the grass, its horn blaring. The truck stopped a few feet from the wounded heap of my body, and my attackers bolted away into the darkness.

The driver helped me onto my feet and into his truck, asking me repeatedly if I was okay. He reached behind his seat and removed a white dress shirt from inside a bag and offered it to me so that I could wipe the blood from my face. Although I initially refused, I ultimately gave in to his insistence, all the while begging him to let me buy him another shirt. He drove me to my car and reluctantly left me to drive myself back home. I never got his name, and I never saw him again.

I drove back to my parents' house in Littleton, where I had been living at the time. The warm smells of dinner lingered as I entered the kitchen to find both my parents sitting at the kitchen table. My mother was mending some clothes and my father, squinting through his bifocals as he perused a pile of bills, peered up from his drudgery. He was the first to see me.

I must have been a nightmarish vision, my head and torso covered in my own blood. The crimson that was spattered and smeared on my face disguised the embarrassment I felt as I inched closer, telling them that I had been mugged. I figured that this version of the story, punctuated by my appearance, would elicit sympathy, but it seemed only to enrage my father, who screamed furiously at me while my mother stood back and stared in shock.

"What the hell were you doing there in the first place?"

This response felt like another brutal kick, and bitter tears swelled inside me like nausea. I needed them to kiss it and make it all better. Instead they made me feel like a child who had just burned the house down while trying to surprise his parents with breakfast in bed. I stammered and tried desperately to come up with some explanation, but my efforts quickly devolved into a violent shouting match between my father and me as my mother cried quietly in the background. There was no way now that I could let them know what had really happened, much less that I *was* the very thing these men despised and tried to destroy. I drove myself to the hospital, the pain in my body muted by the agony of this betrayal.

I spent the next two hours in the hospital's urgent care waiting room, surrounded by crying infants cradled by mothers, and a motley bunch of the sick and injured. I felt a spotlight on me as every broken person in that waiting room stared at my blood-soaked body sitting silently in a corner. A couple of x-rays and a police report later, I was sent on my way.

I did not go back home that night. I could never return to the darkness where I had kept my secret hidden from the oppressive judgments of a Catholic mother and an overbearing father. I could no longer feign interest in the women with whom I had formed ineffectual relationships. The walls I had so carefully constructed around me had collapsed. The hazy light of a new day dawned to reveal a winding path, one that I had feared, but now was forced, to take.

I was twenty-one when the cataracts of fear faded and I saw myself for the first time. The paralyzing fear of "faggot" that had held me face down through my life had lost its grip with one good ass kicking that sent me flying to my feet. As I looked back at my torment from a distance, its monstrous shape no longer seemed as threatening as it had in the past. The fetters of shame had been broken, and now I would need to learn to walk on new, uncertain legs. With a cautious confidence in my steps, I ventured forward and never looked back.

● ● ●

The concept of "family" is one that has been used against GLBT people for decades, and it's a Colorado favorite. The "preservation of the family" involves marriage between a man and a woman only, adoption by a male-parent-female-parent combination only, membership in a church that believes that same-sex attraction can be "cured," and abstaining from sex until marriage—all stipulations that exclude gay men, lesbians, and many bisexual, transgendered, and queer-identified people. Without the ability to marry, for same-sex couples, abstaining from sex until marriage means agreeing to a lifetime of celibacy—something that even the strictest, most conservative, and most observant Evangelical Christians in Colorado have not undertaken.

When "family" applies to everyone but us, and when even our family of origin may not be welcoming, we have a couple of choices—we can give up, renounce who we are, and join Exodus International, or we can take pride in our identity, form our own kinship bonds, and create the concept of "family" on our *own* terms. We like the second option, thank you very much. We only wish that others would focus on their own families at least as much as they do on ours.

Homecoming Out
to James Dean

Debra A. Myers

Debra A. Myers is a post-punk, pierced 'n tattooed poly Leather Femme switch going through her second adolescence in an effort to avoid responsibility and menopause. Her hobbies are reading, writing, film studies, sex ed, BDSM, eating sushi, and wrangling big cats. She lives in Denver, works for an alt newsweekly, and is currently searching for the meaning of life, the perfect spicy tuna hand roll, and a butch/trannyboi Leather Daddy who looks like James Dean.

*L*IKE JAMES DEAN, I grew up in a tiny rural town in Indiana. And like James Dean, I left that small Indiana town as soon as I could. He got out young. After a few false starts, I got out, older. We both dreamed of becoming famous. He made it. I didn't. I never starred on Broadway, in television, or in films. He never made it past the age of 24.

Being raised in Indiana, I had always taken James Dean for granted. His image was so pervasive and his legend so available, I didn't pay it much attention. It wasn't until I moved to Colorado that I rediscovered him.

I came here nine years ago, hoping to escape my natal state's religious Republican mentality—not to mention the multitude of mullet-headed dykes (and het men) who thought that taking your girl out for a swanky night on the town consisted of dinner at Old Country Buffet and a tractor pull. Over the years, one by one, all my friends moved out of state, and I found myself with few like minds left with which to socialize and commiserate. I finally decided it was time to leave the home of the infamous Mr. Potato Head, Dan Quayle, after my ailing father died and my mother moved to Arizona to live with my sister and her family. So I struck out for Denver, where my best gay-boy friend had happily relocated years before.

Once here, I landed a job as the buyer for a lesbian/feminist bookstore, which, if it didn't make me rich, at least paid (most of) my bills and, more importantly, fed my soul. I made some new fabulous friends. I got laid—a lot. For some reason, Rocky Mountain dykes loved me—or maybe my prestigious position at the women's bookstore was the draw.

Colorado was definitely an improvement over Indiana. I was finally able to see myself through new eyes and find a new identity. Later, when I became reacquainted with James Dean, I saw him through new eyes, too.

While doing some research for a story I was writing, I found that Dean was not quite the straight macho stud that Hollywood has positioned him to be. Several sources quoted his reply when asked if he were gay: "Well, I'm certainly not going through life with one hand tied behind my back." He also had documented relationships with influential gay men in Hollywood, and a slew of tell-all books about Dean from some of those purported ex-beaus were starting to hit the stands. Dean was young and possibly still developing his sexuality. I will never know if he was gay, bisexual, or questioning. But I do know that, by the time I had finished my investigation, I had found an unexpected kinship with my home-state boy—just in time for my first pilgrimage back there.

My mother is elderly and in poor health. I hadn't been back to Hoosier-ville since I moved away, but she had returned, and I thought maybe it was time to visit her before I lost the chance. I wasn't looking forward to it. My family and I have never been close and we don't share much personal news. In a pathetic attempt at coming out during a conversation with my mother several years ago, I tossed out a vague reference to my sliding-scale sexuality, mumbling something about moving from a Kinsey 2 to a Kinsey 5. In the time-honored manner of midwestern denial, Mom barked a hysterical laugh and never spoke of it again. Subsequent attempts to convince her that, indeed, I was still dating girls and would probably never go back to dating bio-boys full-time were summarily pooh-poohed and ignored. So I gave up.

For this trip, I prepared carefully. I reserved a hotel room and a rental car to avoid lodging with my staunch Catholic mother and her caretakers, my born-again brother and sister-in-law. I commandeered my best gal-pal, Michelle (in the tried-and-true dyke tradition, she was also my ex-girlfriend) to be my traveling companion for moral support—and to share my visit with James Dean.

As Michelle and I headed for my family's hick-town home, we made a pit stop at the James Dean Gallery, located then in Gas City, Indiana. Plunked down in the never-ending cornfields between a truck stop and a water tower, the James Dean Gallery was nonetheless impressive. Built just the previous year, the shiny new 7400-square-foot, Art Deco–style tile-and-glass-block building housed the world's largest collection of James Dean memorabilia, from film wardrobes and posters to statues, paintings, books, magazines, and an innumerable array of tchotchkes from more than 30 countries. Ranging from the merely quirky to the truly bizarre, there were James Dean T-shirts, ties, and trading cards alongside James Dean Christmas ornaments, cologne, and Cyrillic nesting dolls. And finally, the heartbreaking memorabilia: pieces of his 1955 silver Porsche Spyder 550 and the road sign from the Cholame, California, intersection—the setting for the tragic automobile accident that ended his life.

Michelle and I began by touring the exhibits, taking a break only to park ourselves in the gallery's 35-seat movie theater and watch a 1988 documentary. Though it contained some worthwhile trivia, the film's cheesy '80s power-ballad theme song and its intrusive and petulant homophobic segments—featuring various boyhood friends and relatives testifying as to Dean's rampant heterosexuality—made viewing painful. But the exhibits made the visit worthwhile.

As I examined each object, I felt that I was coming to know Dean intimately. And what I was getting was a strong sense of his "otherness"—his outsider/rebel persona, the boy who never quite fit in. Too intelligent, too artsy, too quiet, too much of a loner, too . . . gay? Definitely too close to my own childhood.

I walked through the aisles, awed to see his letters, his journals, his astonishing original paintings. But the bittersweet tell for me was the photo of tiny Marcus, his weeks-old Siamese kitten—a gift from his friend, budding starlet Elizabeth Taylor—reclining closed-eyed and blissful in the windowsill. Along with the photo was a sheet of meticulously handwritten feeding instructions left for Dean's actress friend Jeanette Miller, who was cat-sitting Marcus on the day Dean drove off to the ill-fated racing trip from which he never returned.

Marcus, who was named after Dean's cousin. Marcus, whose homemade gourmet kitty-food recipe included egg yolk, evaporated milk, and "white Karo" syrup. The kitten-sitter was cautioned, "Don't feed him meat or formula cold," and reminded, in addition to administering his daily vitamin solution, to "Take Marcus to Dr. Cooper's on Melrose for shots next week." Marcus, a Siamese—an exotic cat breed in the '50s, and an unusual and curious pet for a boy from rural Indiana. In my experience growing up there, most red-blooded heterosexual Indiana boys were far more likely to kick cats than to coddle them. And Elizabeth Taylor? Well, she's the Queen Mother of fag hags now, but maybe Jimmy was her first.

Later, I spoke with the gallery owner, a slim but wiry, handsome man with dark hair and glasses, who sported the ubiquitous midwestern male uniform of work boots, jeans, and a plaid flannel shirt. But there was something that set him apart—an educated, articulate outsider air. And despite his age—he was probably somewhere in his mid-50s—he possessed a youthful, well-groomed look. All of that reminded me of Dean.

When he told us about the history of the gallery, he let slip the words "my partner." He lived with his "partner" in a restored 1905 Victorian home in downtown Fairmount, their original gallery location in James Dean's hometown. He ran the gallery with his "partner." His words echoed in my ears. Did he mean business partner, life partner, or both? I suspected the latter. But what could I say or do to make him trust me enough to disclose? Surely he could see that my ex and I were family. But what could I do? Gas City, Indiana, is not exactly the safest place in the world to come out. And what if I was wrong? Out of respect, I kept quiet, even though the question lay unasked and burning on the tip of my tongue as Michelle and I left the gallery.

In the end, all my stress and foreboding about a fire-and-brimstone clash with my family was a false alarm. My mother was in her usual happy-to-see-you, Queen-of-Denial, "Don't Ask, Don't Tell" persona, the one where she conveniently forgets that we have never gotten along, have never understood each other, could never communicate—that our relationship was a study in conflict since the day I developed my own mind—and that was just fine by me.

My brother and sister-in-law were apparently the kinder, gentler type of Christians who didn't proselytize. They gave me—and Michelle—a warm reception. Assuming that she was my current girl-friend, my family treated her as potential relative material. My brother even included Michelle in het-male/butch bonding jokes, and later, she was herded into an extemporaneous family photo shoot without a pause.

When we were joined by my niece and her—second? third? fourth?—husband and their two children of questionable paternity, it was a shock to see how mature and developed and doe-eyed-beautiful my great-nieces were. The oldest one was a high-school sophomore, and I held out a momentary spark of hope for her—she was gothy and artsy, thrilled to show me her sketchbook filled with drawings of fairy and vampire girls in long, flowy RenFair gowns, and she said she liked to torment boys. Perhaps there was a gay gene in my family, after all? We seemed to have an instant rapport, the two black sheep of the family finding solace in our shared outsider status.

All in all, it was a surprisingly non-drama-filled experience and I was glad I'd made the journey. Despite the fact that I hadn't achieved closure with my mother, we'd both been on our best behavior and had managed not to open up old wounds or rip any new ones. It was an oddly satisfying homecoming, though Indiana had never really felt like home to me, and still doesn't. Nonetheless, I was relieved it was over and was looking forward to returning to Colorado, my present home, the next day.

On the drive back to our hotel, I pondered my homecoming—and James Dean. I thought about what we had in common and what we didn't. Would his family have been as hospitable if he'd visited with a boyfriend? Maybe. Would his fans have turned their backs if he'd come out as queer? Probably. Would Hollywood have blacklisted him? Almost certainly. Silently, I looked up at the stars in our Indiana night sky and wished Jimmy a belated welcome into my tribe.

• • •

Even when we choose a "traditional" family structure, we are sometimes thwarted in our efforts. Legislative bills that would allow for two-same-sex-parent adoptions have failed repeatedly over the years, but in the spring of 2007, such a bill was finally passed and signed into law by a new Colorado governor. Now there is nothing to stop us from fulfilling our role as parents if we so decide. We know that loved, wanted, and well-raised children are the future of our state, our country, and our world, and that good parents are good parents, no matter what their respective genders. So those of us who are called will answer—and, as with everything else, we'll do it our way.

Luminaria

LISA LUSERO

Lisa Lusero is the Assistant Director of The Michael Palm Center and a student at the University of Denver College of Law. Her interdisciplinary work is published in The Journal of Democracy and Education, Educational Insights, *and* Revolutionary Voices: A Multicultural Queer Youth Anthology, *including excerpts of her one-woman show,* Impossible Body. *She has worked as a performance artist, a teacher at the Logan School for Creative Learning, and as the Education Director at Deproduction, a grassroots media production company. She is an active volunteer with organizations working for healthy, sustainable communities, including the Chinook Fund and the Colorado Alliance of Independent Midwives. She is a coparent of two children in a two-mom/two-dad family.*

THERE WERE MANY TIMES during the birth of my son that I thought, "I am *so* glad I'm not in a hospital." When I burrowed under a blanket, it was my blanket. When I cranked up the stereo, there was no one to disturb but my neighbors. When I wanted peanut-butter toast at 2 A.M., it was my peanut butter on my bread. Believe it or not, it's the little things that matter when you're stretching your cervix over someone's head.

Let me explain. My partner and I, together with a gay male friend, decided to have kids. We were all twenty-somethings, without retirement plans, stable careers, or big bank accounts. It was a messy time to be starting a family, but a family is a messy thing to be starting, so it made sense to us.

When it was my turn to be pregnant, I knew I would want to have a homebirth. Enter Flame—a fitting name for this dyke midwife. After my labor, a friend who was present described her as "a force of nature," which is definitely something you want on your side when giving birth. We met Flame in my partner's eighth month of pregnancy after some unfulfilling childbirth preparation classes. A friend suggested we talk to a midwife, and in one meeting, she did what no hospital tour, *What to Expect When You're Expecting,* or physiological road map could do—she made my partner feel like a champion, like she alone could give birth to the world, or at the very least, this baby.

It became clear that when my partner went into labor we would want Flame there. Though the plan was still to end up at the hospital, we were in no rush to get there. Flame helped us navigate the unfamiliar zone of labor on our own. My partner labored for twenty hours, seventeen of them at home. After our first son was born, we both felt like Flame's presence was invaluable and absolutely altered the course of events for the better. This experience sealed it—for me, childbirth would be at home all the way.

Making the nontraditional choice has been a common theme in my life, and the birth of my child was no time to concede to the dominant paradigm—no time to concede anything. Being pregnant and in labor was one of the most profoundly vulnerable experiences of my life. The last thing I wanted to do was be in an unfamiliar environment, where my queer family would have to be explained and my radical energy would have to be contained. The fact that only one percent of Colorado babies are born at home was undaunting. Beyond gut instinct, there are plenty of reasons why a healthy woman would be better off giving birth at home.

Instead of a half-hour of waiting room fun, followed by peeing and perusal of vitals with a brief opportunity for questions (on a good day), with Flame I got to spend up to an hour and a half talking *at each prenatal appointment.* Not only did I feel physically well cared for, but all of my questions were answered and all of my fears were reckoned with. I felt like Flame was a partner, an advocate, and a mentor. Planning a homebirth was about bringing to labor the integrity and wholeness that I bring to myself, my baby, my family, and the miracle of life.

Still, by the time I went into labor, I was terrified. Thrilled and excited and terrified. The process of planning a homebirth required so much forethought and organizing that I knew everything that could be in place was. Loved ones were present. Family was notified. The space was prepared. Supplies were in line. Luminarias—flaming candles in paper bags—surrounded the house. Flame had arrived. The only thing left to do was dive into the unknown. Align myself with the tides of life and death. Labor. Birth. Yes, there was pain. But the pain didn't compare to the fear.

Nine o'clock at night—Flame tells me I am two centimeters dilated. No way around it; two centimeters was not enough. It meant a day's worth of nauseating contractions got me nowhere. It was like hiking all day and then coming to the trailhead. The most difficult stretch was looming in the distance. There was no choice but to continue to begin. The night became a dance—the face of my partner, the hands of my compañera, the voice of Flame, the rhythm of my brother's drumming, the breath of la familia, the heat of the rooms. I dove and dove and lost perspective, found my demons, growled at myself. I was scared, angry, lonely—and home.

At one point I grabbed a copy of *Sister Outsider* by Audre Lorde and opened it to my favorite essay. I was looking for a sentiment that could contain my anger and give me something to hold on to through the pain. There are lots of good lines, but this one jumped out and became my mantra that night: "And it is a grave responsibility. Projected from within each of us. Not to settle for the convenient, the shoddy, the conventionally expected, nor the merely safe." In retrospect, this was a perfect mantra for labor. It is our own capacity for joy that we are responsible to. If we honor the fear, the pain, the anger, we also honor our joy. Birthing at home was about making choices to honor all of this, to recognize labor as not merely a physical feat, but a human rite.

Eventually, time lost all meaning. My world was nothing more than the powerful women holding me, the drumming of my brother, and pain. Then out of nowhere, my guts turned into a lion, and the strength to push raged through me in waves.

"That's how hard you have to work to push this baby out," Flame said.

Whimpering and pleading turned to hollering. Just when it seemed impossible, a wild surge pierced my muscles. Daybreak. I was pushing my baby out, burning, like the Colorado sun splitting open the morning sky. Head. Body. Flesh. Then the lion was gone, the room was full, the house was full, there was light. Our baby had been born.

The Patron Saint of Midwives should be a lesbian. There is a profound love of women present in the energy of labor and in the witnessing of birth. For Flame, a love of women is the foundation of her practice, and that spirit pervaded my experience. Homebirth isn't a lesbian issue, but if anyone should tune in to this sphere of woman-loving-woman juice, it should be us.

• • •

Colorado's GLBT population is as diverse and varied as our landscape. We may have many things in common as a group, but we are also individuals, each with our own quest to formulate and solidify our own identity, our individual family, and our immediate community. We want to find our own place and our own people within the much larger group. And Colorado is ideal for that, because the state's queer community offers a variety of support, services, and activities that acknowledge individualized needs within the whole—places to go and things to do that are ethnicity-, age-, gender-, faith-, and interest-specific.

But even with the vast array of specialized groups and activities, we still have to discover where we fit within the Colorado GLBT community, which is so large and so diverse that it sometimes establishes its own criteria for inclusion—both within the umbrella group and within the various factions that naturally form under it. Does the T belong with GLB? Where do bisexual people fit? In what order should the letters go? Identity politics may sometimes be problematic, but it will exist as long as there are separate identities to be carved out, which will probably be forever—because our community is not a monolith, and that's the way we like it.

Bodies, Borders, and Battles

NICK SARCHET

*Nick Sarchet is a social justice advocate and activist living in Denver
with his son AJ. Born to very lucky parents in Las Vegas, Nick was raised
in Michigan as a girl named Kim. Through an unlikely journey that took
her from a small rural town to a stint in the army, time as a corrections
officer in a state penitentiary, a marriage, and the birth of her son, Kim
eventually came out as a big ole dyke and, in time, as transgender. Once
living as a guy, Nick realized that label didn't really fit either and now
proudly claims queer as his political, sexual, and gender identity.*

*Nick currently pays the bills as a consultant and trainer for Agility
Results, a business he started for himself in 2005. After 10 years in the
nonprofit arena, Nick is passionate about assisting progressive
organizations in their ability to adapt, grow, and succeed. His Web site is
www.agilityresults.com. In his free time, Nick loves scuba diving,
spending time with AJ, and sharing good times with his close-knit
community.*

(This piece was written at and inspired by Denver's hottest spoken word
set, Café Nuba.)

> *While I create and re-create my identity, my body, my being,*
> * you create the borders.*
> *Divisions of race; separation of classes; partitioning of queer*
> * identities . . .*
> *One box is not enough for my life*
> *White, queer, privileged, oppressed—trying to find the space I fit*
> *Scratching out a place within the GLBT—facing more battles*

Scratching out a place within the trans community? A community
I thought was my own.
More borders, more boxes.
Shrinking my identity to fit into someone else's definition?
  Crossdresser? Drag queen? Bigender? Transgender?
    Transsexual?
  Wait, that's not enough!
      Non-op
        Pre-op
          Post-op
            FTM
              MTF
Be more of a man, be more of a woman.
But what makes a man? What makes a woman?
Society's setting up borders and more borders. Calling in the
  border patrol, telling me don't cross this line, don't claim this
  identity . . . it's already taken.

  But who defines the terms?
You see, I am not your vision of the straight chick—feminist
woman who can handle it all.
  Work a job, birth a child, feed the family, and take care of my
  man.
  Although . . . for nine months my belly did carry a child,
    and these breasts, now removed, fed him daily for quite
    a while.

And I am not to be put in your dyke box—a butch icon with the
  scent of a woman on one hand and a tool box in the other.
  Although . . . the scent of the right woman has seduced me
    to fix a sink or two.

*And I am not your notion of the straight dude—9 to 5 job, shave
and cologne, remote control, chugging beers with the boys.
Although . . . like it or not, I often receive the "good ole
boy" treatment.*

*And I don't fit your gay boy box either—hot hung Top, looking
for Bottom; no fats, no femmes.
Although . . . with the right equipment, I can be as hung as
you want me to be.*

*And I am certainly not your preconception of the transsexual—
six-foot guy in a dress, broad shoulders, five o'clock shadow,
neatly moving from one gender box to the next.
Although . . . at one time, I thought I had to.*

*So who do you think I am now?
Does my body frighten you?
Repulse you?
Intrigue you?
Turn you on?*

*You see, the person you thought you saw when you looked at me
was your perception, your shit,
trying to cram me in a box that doesn't fit.
You need to peel back the layers, look beyond my outer skin—
find the true identities that lie within.*

*bodies, Bodies, BODIES!
My sisters, my brothers, my sister-brothers, my brother-sisters.
I am just trying to create language here! Language for bodies,
identities, individualities that do not fit within your
contentions, your definitions, your limitations.*

Bodies beaten and bloody for crossing these gender borders.
  Averaging 13 deaths per year and, shit, those are just the ones
    we know about.
    Invisible, throw-away community, bodies not their own
      property, trying to conform to society.
        They are gender warriors fighting for their survival.

Hell . . . I am fighting for survival.
  The freedom to create, to fulfill, to express true identity

I am my own person—stretched and pulled, poked and punched
  by a society trying to knead me, form me into something
  recognizable, acceptable, and comprehendible. Stick me in a
  box. I'll still raise an identity. Beat me back down and I will
  rise again and again.

I determine my identity—I am the only one who has survived
  my life.

● ● ●

stoplights read
RED ORANGE YELLOW

ALYSHA WOOD

Alysha Wood is a mixed, queer and otherly gendered writer, dancer, and performing artist currently pursuing an MFA in writing and poetics at Naropa University in Boulder, Colorado. Editor of Tendrel, *Naropa's diversity journal, she is creating a body of performances around her current manuscript, which focuses on immigration, transit, and translation across borders of genealogy and gender. She received a BA interdisciplinary degree in Asian Studies, Creative Writing, and Dance from Hollins University in Roanoke, Virginia, and has been published in* Glimpse Abroad *online,* The Charleston Gazette, *and several small literary journals. She continues to curate the blog TRANS/VERSE: critical responses to bordered bodies in word, film, performance, and sound at www.eucalyptusraven.blogspot.com.*

(A spoken word text written for the demise of the three-year-old Bachelor of Fine Arts in Performance program at Naropa University, Boulder, Colorado, Spring 2006. Dedicated to ex-chair Pearl Ubungen, ex-faculty Edris Cooper-Anifowoshe, and all the students.)

stoplights read RED ORANGE YELLOW
High Alert is no comfort
when The Airport confiscates our shoes,
searches our eyes for an excuse to distrust the thrust of our lives

High Alert is no comfort
when the Auction Block sings
with the sting of our skin
Our People bartered off for Green

while "Go" is an Untranslatable Transaction
whose meaning dissolves in Reaction
could you eliminate this Contraction
unless you want an Un-American Faction
to fly your flag upside down
because blood proceeds all stars of good deeds
and Ignorance is not Innocence
IGNORANCE IS NOT INNOCENCE
but a Fence against all Dark Daughters

you say
Immigrants are Criminal
Criminal is Immigrant
and the Institutional Sentence is
Genocide because you won't ever let us Decide

if your Request for Student Voice is just for Show
then I'm tired of being an Exhibitionist
in your World's Fair
because it isn't fa(i)re to still pay the price of Discrimination
this Crime Nation can Racialize Genderize and Tenderize me
until I'm All Eyes to the Television Commercial of what you want
        me to see

I bite the bridal bit with my teeth
as you construct Meat Markets online
where men can buy Thai Brides
and European models advertise
Healthy White Skin Lotion
for all Brown Notions
and message boards exotify
The Mixed Asian Girl mummified
Yeah, let us Infiltrate your Wet Dream—
you can't figure out what we are

in this Desperate Desert of Perverts and Hermits
of Floating Heads sucking
the earth dry for Spiritual Awakening
you tell me to Keep Drinking Water Keep Drinking Water
  KEEP DRINKING WATER
in this Mile-High Elevation of Starvation
Arapahoe Avenue
paved over the Aboriginal
so we no longer know Ground
STOP Climbing Ladders to WATER ME DOWN

this is a TERRORTRAUMATERRORTRAUMATERRORTRAUMA
  world
where drama is on ER and BLACKWHITE face paint is an
  Other mask of hate
EMERGENCY! the TV dictates periphery
heightens respectability for all modes of surgery
"I'm Sorry, Unless Your InsUrgency is Completely Necessary"—
we suggest you release your hands from our throats
and let us choke on your joke of "Commitment to Diversity"
  ENDQUOTE!

I'd like to VOTE
but of course the ballot's stashed
masquerading in a circus parade raiding
of Input, Impact and Persuasion
as if your Invasion could acquiesce our Exclusion
as if your Invasion could pass for Nonviolent Communication

You want Us to "Make an Appointment"
before our Internment
before you Slaughter all our children
did you answer One Question
or is this a Competition

to see whose rendition of Democracy best fits your Definition
and if you'd finish this Pattern of Repetition
you'll find the Mission Statement, World Wisdom Traditions
all Cultural Appropriations of Property Divisions
Dis-solutions Dis-illusions and Fabrication

you expect us to rise to our Ex-Potential
without the Exponential value of
Post-Colonial Inscriptions, Transruptions and Petitions
invoking higher Amalgamations of Fruition
did you forget the Woman who Died for this Position?

go ahead, Pull Up a Cushion
while you do all that Mental Masturbation
let this be your Contemplative Education:
Am I Walking the Walk? Am I Talking the Talk?
because I didn't see you stand by the BFA
as they painted themselves with blood on
Community Practice Day

the community I practice involves
getting up and moving
involves fighting injustice and the usual statement of
"I can't hear you if you're angry"

You Want Us to Use Right Speech
To Transcend This Rage
Come to a Place of Non-Attachment to Emotion
I'm certain this incessant Devotion is murdering my Passion
what happened to FREE SPEECH
WHAT HAPPENED TO FREE SPEECH

we are called Terrorist when we Resist
WE ARE CALLED TERRORIST WHEN WE RESIST
and I Insist to use my Fist to stick
a Post-It on your Door
4's the Score and 20 years of death by your hands,
swept under an Interim of Cuts, Can'ts and Cancellations
as you put up Demarcations against our Demonstrations
and is that Information you can't Tell us because it's
Confidential?

we Colored are Colonized by Confidential Files
a Wall between the U.S. and all its Lies
soon you'll burn the Witch, the Queer,
because you still can't figure out what we are

we live on a floodplain
but what about the bloodstains
and who feels this pain
this is a Revolution
we are all Arising in Connection
the Birth of three White Buffalo lets us know
the old ways are returning

I say the Body is a Site of Resistance
and this is just One Instance
of how we'll Prevail

• • •

No matter who we are, no matter where we fit—or don't—Colorado is as good a place as any—and better than most—to make those discoveries. In our history, in our land, in our loves, and even in the faces of those who oppose us, we see everything that we can be—and it's more than enough.

Time Elastic

DARONA DRAKA

darona draka is a poet and artist who lives with her wife, a small fluffy dog, and a gang of protecting dragons who have helped her heal from deep life traumas. In her spare time, she is an attorney helping GLBT people in Denver to talk about and plan for illness and death.

Time elastic,
my heart and soul and mind are
whipped into a racing
pace across the Rocky Mountain passes
by the winter wind that launches
powder snow into its trusted air and
space beyond the cliffs to soar and
dance across the brilliant snowline
slashing through a blue so bright it
cuts into my vision like a
hawk's
shrill
piercing
cry.

This strange and brittle
landscape holds some
power for me but the
light is too intense for me to
see the consequences

laid before my
sight.

I watch the hawks and snowflakes,
marvel at their lust for
flight and freedom from
my need to
hold to solid ground.

I'm not sure whether
soaring in this
brilliant blue brings
salve or brittle shards of glass.
I do not know the path but
follow to the
edge
prepared to
leap
since
flying is the
only
safe
way
out and I must learn to
trust the
lack of ground
beneath my
feet.

    ● ● ●

A Journey Through the Looking Glass

LILY MARLOWE

Lily Marlowe was born on September 22, 1954, in Denver, Colorado. She has a birth certificate issued by the State of Colorado showing her name as Lilian Grace Marlowe and her gender as female. This is the second birth certificate issued to her by the state. The first one had a boy's name on it and said she was male. Since November 15, 2005, she has been legally and anatomically female.

One of Lily's earliest observations about her culture was that little boys are often asked, "What do you want to be when you grow up?" Common answers included "Policeman," "Fireman," and "Cowboy." She wonders how many of those little boys really just wanted to grow up to be a member of The Village People.

She knew in her heart that her one and only true answer to that question was, "I want to grow up to be a woman." She ascertained very early on that she dare not utter those words aloud, so she proceeded to create and live her entire childhood and adolescence deep in her imagination, where she was, of course, a girl. Finally, her biggest dream came to fruition. She grew up to be a woman.

Dear Loving Friends,

I apologize sincerely for what you are about to read. I could think of no other way to communicate this information to you. I have finally reached resolution surrounding an issue with which I have been grappling all of my life. Lately, I feel myself sinking deeply into madness once again, and I fear that I shall not recover this time. I don't want to recover this time.

I have reached the end of my long and painful journey, so I am doing what seems to be the best thing to do, to carry out a plan I have harbored for longer than I can remember—to facilitate my own demise.

All of you have given me the greatest possible happiness that is available to a soul such as me. You have all been, in every way, everything that one can be to a fellow human being. I know that I am, in a very significant way, causing you great anguish. I know also that I am spoiling the rich and life-affirming part of our lives that brought us much happiness and fulfillment. Without me, you will be free to pursue the goals in your life unencumbered.

What I want to convey to you is that I owe all of the happiness of my life to each and every one of you. Everything is gone from me but the certainty of your goodness, your love, and your divine light. I cannot go on spoiling your lives any longer. I have become an anchor for your hearts—one that no human being should have to bear.

The fact that I have been unable to remedy my situation through prayer, meditation, medication, or hospitalization is, I think, a sign that I have fulfilled my purpose on this earth and it is my time to move on to the next realm. I have reached a point in my life at which there is nowhere else to go.

The method I have chosen is really immaterial. I do, however, assure you that I have done extensive research on the Internet and found a way that will be quick. I will feel no pain. And it will most assuredly be final. I implore you to understand that this is not a proverbial cry for help; rather it is a clear proclamation of intention.

I request that there be no formal memorial service. I pray that each of you will remember me in your own special way. I know that I am loved deeply, and I shall cherish each and every one of you in perpetuity. Unfortunately, love is insufficient to sustain me in this, my final hour of despair. I surrender to my ultimate fate. The very life force that flows through me shall transfer to all of you. In this way, I shall live on forever—as shall we all. I love you all madly. I'll miss you dreadfully.

I set myself free.

THAT WAS MY SUICIDE NOTE. And it's obvious, since I am writing this, that I didn't kill myself. But I did set myself free.

I am a female who was born with a birth defect—a penis. I have come to believe that I must have an angel (or two) watching over me, because as often as I have wanted to kill myself, I am still here. I decided that there was another option.

I began female hormones in 1998. I would undergo years of painful and expensive laser and electrolysis treatments to get rid of my facial hair. In 2005, I made the trip to San Francisco for facial feminization surgery—a new nose, an upper lip lift, the removal of massive amounts of jawbone as well as the adjoining musculature, a chin implant, and a brow lift. I also got two shaves—the brow ridge on my forehead and my Adam's apple—and all for only $40,000.

When I returned to Denver, the effects were immediately obvious, although it would take several months for the swelling to dissipate. That was the quintessential "step through the looking glass." From that point on, no one *ever* perceived me to be anything other than a woman. It changed my life—forever.

Then it was time to go to Trinidad, Colorado—the sex change capital of the world. My surgery took four-and-a-half hours—and $20,000 from my bank account. But I finally felt complete—free from the prison in which I had been held captive for over 50 years. I was finally finished—or so I thought. But "no job is finished until the paperwork's done."

Now that I have legally established my new identity, my money is almost gone and I must begin to generate some income very soon. I'm terrified of this prospect after being out of the workforce for over two years. All I have to do is walk out my front door and go. But that first step is going to be the hardest.

I may be scared, but I *can* say that my biggest dream has come to fruition. How many people can say that? It may be a daunting process—to go back out into the world and start life over at 52. But . . . I shall be doing it as Lilian Grace Marlowe—woman.

I set myself free.

• • •

The sound of freedom—to be who we are, just as we are, with equal rights for all—resonates throughout our state, thanks to Colorado's many GLBT voices. May the glorious noise never end.

Resources

There are literally hundreds of groups, organizations, and support systems for GLBT people in Colorado—far too many to list here. If you live here, you probably know them. But if this book convinced you to investigate our wonderful state, visit, or even move here, we offer a few of our many resources to get you started. From there, you will be directed to whatever you might need.

Centers

Boulder Pride (groups, resources, programs, and support in the Boulder area since 1994): 303-499-5777, www.boulderpride.org.

Gender Identity Center of Colorado (groups, resources, programs, and support for the gender community since 1978): 303-202-6466, www.gicofcolo.org.

GLBT Community Center of Colorado—The Center (groups, resources, programs, and support in Denver and beyond since 1976): 303-733-7743, www.glbtcolorado.org.

Lambda Community Center (groups, resources, programs, and support in the Fort Collins/northern Colorado area since 1996): 970-221-3247, www.lambdacenter.org.

Pikes Peak Gay and Lesbian Community Center (groups, resources, programs, and support in the Colorado Springs/southern Colorado area since 1978): 719-471-4429, www.ppglcc.org.

Western Equality (groups, resources, programs, and support in the Grand Junction/Western Slope area since 1992): 970-242-8949, www.westernequality.org.

HIV/AIDS

Boulder County AIDS Project (services for the Boulder area): 303-444-6121, www.bcap.org.

Colorado AIDS Project (services for the Denver area and beyond): 303-837-0166, www.coloaidsproject.org.

Northern Colorado AIDS Project (services for the Fort Collins/ northern Colorado area): 970-484-4469, www.ncaids.org.

Southern Colorado AIDS Project (services for the Colorado Springs/Pueblo/southern Colorado area): 719-561-2616, www.s-cap.org.

Western Colorado AIDS Project (services for the Grand Junction/ Western Slope area): 970-243-2437, www.westcap.info.

Online

Café Vivid (online guide to GLBT Colorado): www.cafevivid.com.

Fort Pride (online guide for Fort Collins/northern Colorado): www.fortpride.org.

Southern Colorado Equality Alliance (resources and events for Pueblo/southern Colorado): www.socoequality.org.

Publications

Colorado Pride Guide (a Colorado business, travel, relocation, recreation, and entertainment resource for the GLBT community): 303-377-1826, gayrockies@aol.com, www.gaycolorado.com.

Denver Pink Pages: 303-316-4688, www.pinkmag.com/Denver.

Out Front Colorado (Colorado's oldest and most widely read GLBT publication since 1976): 303-778-7900, www.outfrontcolorado.com.

Weird Sisters West (Colorado's oldest lesbian-owned publication since 1991): 303-895-7408, 970-416-1251, www.weirdsisters.org.

Services

CLIP (The Center's Legal Initiatives Project): 303-733-7743, www.glbtcolorado.org.

Colorado Anti-Violence Program (crisis intervention and 24-hour emergency assistance for GLBT victims of violence in Colorado; training and education for organizations): 303-839-5204, 24-hour crisis hotline: 303-852-5094, 888-557-4441, www.coavp.org.

Colorado Business Council (GLBT Chamber of Commerce): 303-595-8042, www.coloradobusinesscouncil.com.

Equal Rights Colorado (statewide lobbying and political activist group): www.equalrightscolorado.org.

PFLAG (Parents, Families and Friends of Lesbians and Gays): go to www.pflag.org to find various chapters in Colorado.

Project Angel Heart (meals for those living with life-threatening illnesses in Denver and Colorado Springs): 303-830-0202, www.projectangelheart.org.

Youth

Inside/Out Youth Services (youth support and activities in the Colorado Springs/southern Colorado area): 719-328-1056, www.insideoutys.org.

Rainbow Alley (youth drop-in center and activities in the Denver area, a program of The Center): 303-733-7743, www.glbt colorado.org.

Acknowledgments

THE EDITOR WOULD LIKE TO THANK Johnson Books for their support of this historic project; Drew Wilson for his patience, input, help, support, and ability to suffer in silence; Greg Wharton, Ian Philips, Michael Brewer, Pat Steadman, Phil Nash, and Deb Pollock for their emergency responses; Greg Montoya, Jay Klein, and *Out Front Colorado* for their help and support; and all of the fantastic contributors who shared their time and talent in the creation of this permanent piece of Colorado GLBT history.

Photos courtesy of *Out Front Colorado,* photographer George Hooper, and Matt Kailey.

About the Editor

MATT KAILEY IS A SPEAKER, AUTHOR, AND TRAINER focusing on issues of gender identity and sexual orientation. He is the author of Lambda Literary Award finalist *Just Add Hormones: An Insider's Guide to the Transsexual Experience* (Beacon Press, 2005), and his work has appeared in the Lambda Award–winning anthology *I Do/ I Don't: Queers on Marriage* (Suspect Thoughts Press, 2004), edited by Greg Wharton and Ian Philips; *From the Inside Out: Radical Gender Transformation, FTM and Beyond* (Manic D Press, 2004), edited by Morty Diamond; *Bisexuality and Transgenderism: Inter-SEXions of the Others* (Harrington Park Press, 2003), edited by Jonathan Alexander and Karen Yescavage; *The Journal of Bisexuality; 5280; Transgender Tapestry;* and *Best Transgender Erotica* (Cleis Press, 2003).

He has also appeared in three films: *Matt Kailey: A Conversation;* Kaiser Permanente's *Our Lives;* and the award-winning *Call Me Malcolm.*

A Denver "transplant" since 1990, he is the staff writer for *Out Front Colorado,* Colorado's oldest and most widely read GLBT publication. He can be reached through his Web site at www.mattkailey.com.

Contributor Lily Marlowe
finally set herself completely free
on March 5, 2007.
Her suicide is a tragic reminder of
the prejudice and discrimination that transpeople
continue to face every day in our society,
but her voice will carry on
in these pages.